Judge Parker & Bass Reeves

Two fisted justice

Book three of the Bass Reeves trilogy

Copyright © 2014 Fred Staff
Graphic Design by Qolla Studio
All rights reserverd
ISNB-10: 149447722X
EAN-13: 9781494477226

Dedication

The Bass Reeves Series is dedicated to:

Royce Peterson, retired Professor of History at the University of Central Oklahoma;
Jack Scammahorn, my longtime friend and fellow teacher;
Bob Brousseau, my wise old friend who has encouraged me strongly in all aspects of life's journey;
Dennis Hambright, who has continually encouraged me in my writing efforts; and
Gypsy Hogan, who has been a tremendous encouragement to me and of great assistance to this project.

Facts

- Bass Reeves was born a slave in Arkansas
- He was raised just outside of Paris, Texas
- His master became the Speaker of the House of state of Texas
- The three battles of the Civil War described are exactly as happened.
- Most of the arrest and conflicts as described in this Trilogy were taken from the official records.
- He escaped into Indian Territory and lived there until he purchased a farm in Van Buren, Arkansas.
- He could speak five tribal languages.
- He was a must requested guide for lawman seeking those that fled to Indian Territory to escape the law.
- When Judge Parker was appointed to the Fort Smith federal district by President Grant he was authorized two hundred marshals to clean up the violent and uncontrolled area known as Indian Territory, now known as Oklahoma and western Arkansas. This area covers over seventy-three thousand square miles, the largest Federal District ever to exist.
- Bass Reeves was one of the first chosen, due to his unmatched ability on tracking and knowledge of the area.
- He never learned to read or write, yet continually arrested the correct person.
- Reeves served for over thirty two years as a US Marshal.
- He arrested over three thousand lawbreakers.
- Bass Reeves was friends with Pistol Peter, Sam Sixkiller, Belle Starr, Bud Ledbetter, and Judge Parker.
- His life's accomplishments have been honored by Arkansas, Oklahoma, The Nation Cowboy Hall of Fame, the Cities of Muskogee, Oklahoma, Fort Smith, Arkansas and Paris, Texas.
- There is an impressive statue t in his honor located in Fort Smith, Arkansas.
- His portrait hangs in many museums and in the states Attorney General's office in Oklahoma.
- It has been rumored that the cartoon character "The Lone Ranger" was based on his adventures.

Chapter 1

Dillard

It was a hot miserable day, not unlike many days of summer in Indian Territory, when Bass and Cliff Culvert, his posse man, rode into town. They tied their horses to a hitching post in the shade and made sure there was adequate water in the trough for their sweating horses to relieve their thirst.

"Cliff, why don't you walk down the right side of the street, and I'll take the left. Let's see who we can flush out of this place."

"Sounds like as good a plan as I know, and 'sides, I need to stretch my legs and get a beer. I'm dry as a bone."

"I guess the good thing about our business is that the people we look for generally hang in places that provide you with refreshment. But be careful. You know that we can't ever let our guard down. I'm sorry if I sound like your mother, but I've come too close to bein' surprised lately and just want everyone to be cautious."

"Bass, it's no problem. We all need to keep thinkin' of each other. I've lost too many good men to let each other get lazy."

Bass turned and crossed the street. The heat was keeping people in place, and the lack of movement was a testament to how much the people were seeking anyplace that provided them an escape from the sweltering heat. It seemed that in the Territory, the heat was often made worse by a wind that made it feel like it was trying to lift your skin off the bone.

Bass entered Cap Shy's General Store, taking off his hat and wiping the sweat from the inside with his bandana. Then he mopped his brow. He strolled slowly toward the back of the store, feeling that Cap would be sitting in his rocker and trying to stir up as much air movement as he could.

When Bass turned the corner, all he could see was the top of Cap's balding head as it moved back and forth with the movement of the rocker.

Bass asked, "Got any good deals today?"

Cap turned, startled at the sound of a voice. It was evident that he had slipped into a dazed mode in an effort to escape the unbearable heat.

"Damn, you caught me cat nappin'. I hadn't had a soul in here in an hour and had just dosed off. What yah doin' in town Bass? Lookin' for people or shade?"

"Well, the shade is welcome, but I got a passel of warrants, and it seems they just keep pilin' up if we don't keep at it. How you doin' Cap?"

"This damned heat is drivin' everybody indoors, so business is slow, but I got what they need, and it'll pick up when it cools. Bass, how's your business? I know when I see you that you're on the lookout for someone. I can't imagine anyone bein' out in this heat without good cause."

"Times is tough, and people keep wantin' to do what they ain't supposed to do," Bass said.

"We sure ain't got no shortage of skunks in this chicken house," Cap responded.

"Seems like the more we take in, it just leaves room for more to come in. But that keeps me busy and I like that."

"How you been? Had any close calls lately?" Cap asked.

"Seems like I have one most anytime I go out. You know, they are a postin' signs all over the place tellin' me that if I show my face, they're goin' to send me home in a box. I keep all of them I find. Gettin' to be a right smart collection. But that's just part of the job. They got their wants and I got mine."

Bass laid a stack of warrants on top of the counter and asked, "Cap, you seen any of these fellers?"

Cap stood and pulled his glasses down from his forehead as he walked to the counter. He thumbed through the papers, and, from time to time, would stop as if he were trying to recall a certain name. He finally pulled two out from the cluster and said, "These two fellers are here in town. If I was a bettin' man, I'd say they is in the saloon cross the street wettin' their whistles."

"Cliff's over there now, and I best go see if I can give 'im a hand."

Cap said, "Fore you go, it nearly slipped my mind, but yesterday, early in the mornin', that feller they call Snake was in here, and he bought more supplies than one man should need. In fact, he bought enough for several men. He rides with Bob Dillard from time to time, and I just thought you might want to know that."

These words stopped Bass in his tracks, and he turned back toward Cap.

"Got any idea where he went?"

"I was out on the porch when he left town, and he was headed west.

Don't know if that helps, but hope it does."

Bass stood in silence for a moment. He stroked his mustache, then said, "I appreciate the tip, and I have an idea that somethin' is a cookin'. When does that train come through here on the way to McAlester? It is about the end of the month, and those miners in Krebs is gonna need paid. Wonder if they might be sendin' the payroll down there?"

"It should be here 'bout noon tomorrow."

Bass questioned, "Takes it 'bout two hours to get from Tulsa to here, right?"

"Yep."

"Cap, I better get goin'. Thanks for the help."

"Any time Bass. Be careful."

As Bass stepped onto the boardwalk in front of the General Store, he saw Cliff leaving the saloon across the street with two men in manacles. Bass quickly moved into the blazing sunlight and rushed across the street.

Cliff saw him coming. "No need for you to hurry. I got these here fellers under control," he told Bass.

"I see that, but we've a problem. What I need for you to do is let 'em go."

"Bass, why would I wanna do that? We got warrants on 'em, and they is the right fellers."

"I know Cliff, but they're small time, and it would take us too long to get 'em back to the wagon. We need to be gettin' on the trail. I got a hunch somethin' big is 'bout to happen, and we don't wanna miss out on it. So let 'em go, and let's get out of here."

Cliff's captives were swaying from all the coolant they had consumed, but they had big smiles on their faces as they heard the exchange between the two lawmen. The men broke out in laughter when Cliff complied with Bass' request.

Cliff told the two, "You were lucky today, but I'll be back."

As they walked to the horses Bass further explained. "We can get 'em anytime. I have a feelin' that Bob Dillard's about to make a play on the train from Tulsa to McAlester. I don't know why, but I just feel it."

"I been with you too many times to start doubtin' you now," Cliff said. "If you feel it, we better get somethin' goin'. What you got on your mind?"

"Let's head to Tulsa. We got time to get to the station and come down the track on the train. If they strike — and I just kinda know they will — we'll be right there on the train waitin' for 'em."

"Sounds like a right smart move to me. Let's get goin'," Cliff said.

***

Once in Tulsa, the two men went directly to the rail station. The stationmaster was about to leave for the evening and seemed somewhat disturbed that his trip home was being interrupted.

Bass introduced himself and presented his papers to the stationmaster. He then told of his suspicions. This revelation totally changed the stationmaster's attitude.

After some hesitancy, the stationmaster confirmed that the train would be carrying the Krebs payroll, a confirmation that made Bass even more confident that his hunch was correct.

Bass convinced the stationmaster to connect an empty cattle car to the train so that he and Cliff could put their horses on board and make the trip in case his suspicions were accurate.

The stationmaster did as instructed, then said, "You know, I now recognize who you are. I've read about you in the paper, but are you sure that you don't need some help?"

"I promise you that we can handle this matter," Bass said. "We've come a long ways in this terrible heat to stop anythin' from happenin' to your train, and we can back it up."

The next morning, with the stationmaster by his side, Bass told the engineer to sound the train's whistle if anything tried to stop the train, and that he and Cliff would take care of matters from there.

The engineer looked at him as if to say, "What's new? We get hit about once every three or four months." However, he told Bass, "I hope you is as good as I hear. I really would like to stop gettin' pistols pushed in my face."

"Might be nothin' happens, but I promise if it does, we'll handle it," Bass told him.

***

Cliff and Bass settled into the cattle car, each taking a position on a stack of hay. They figured that the trip would not be eventful for several miles, so they might as well relax and get prepared for whatever events they hoped they would encounter in the near future.

Both men had checked their weapons and ammunition before entering the train, but as a further precaution, they went through the motions one more time. If Bob Dillard and his gang showed up, they didn't want any malfunction to hinder their efforts to bring this canker to justice.

"How do you like that Henry?" Bass asked, nodding toward Cliff's gun. "I hear a lot of good things about 'em."

"They is a right fine piece of work, but it takes a long time to load 'em," Cliff said. "Course, once yah got that done, yah can lay down more fire than any man should have to. If you is that poor a shoot, might be best if you carried a scatter gun. I can sure see how they were a wonder in the Indian wars, where you got bunches of people wantin' to take your scalp."

Two fisted justice

As the train lumbered along, the men's conversational efforts lessened and time seemed to stand still. At the same time, both men's alertness heightened. They hoped they were approaching a situation that would be not only rewarding to them, but a relief to the Territory.

Bass said, "Cliff, you know I had a chance to get this scoundrel once and only got my horse killed for the effort. Had a sour leg for about a week and had to walk to Pawnee. I really want this guy. I feel he owes me personally. I know the court wants 'im, but not half as bad as I do."

Cliff thought about Bass' words as he felt the warm breeze seep through the slats in the cattle car as he listened to the clicking and clacking of the train as it progressed. Finally, he turned to Bass and asked, "What happened, Bass?"

"I got this tip that he was goin' to be in Pawnee to try to cheat some feller on a land deal, so I sent word to Heck Thomas to meet me there. The trip was long, and I had left Blaze at the prison wagon, 'cause he was favorin' his right leg. Took my posse man's horse and high tailed it to Pawnee. I got there just in time to see Dillard try to make the deal, and I'd been stupid enough not to inform the barkeep that I was a marshal. When I tried to arrest Dillard and his sidekick, the barkeep pulled a shotgun on me and let them get away. He had ever right to because he thought that I was just somebody tryin' to cause problems. But never the less, it let Dillard and his buddy get gone and ahead of me. I trailed 'em, and Dillard left his man to bushwhack me. Lucky for me, he only killed my horse and put a hole in my clothes.

"If Heck would've got there sooner, we may of got 'em, but I guess it was just meant to be that I was gonna have to wait for a day like today to bring this feller down. I sure hope I've guessed right, and we ain't wastin' our time."

"I do, too," Cliff said. "You say you sent word to Heck to back you up. Did he show?"

"Yep, he showed, but a little late. I had already walked back to town by the time he got there. Said he was late in gettin' the message."

Cliff smiled and shook his head. "Bass, yah sure he was late 'cause of that? Yah know he might not have got good feelin's 'bout black folks. All of his family was officers in the Confederate army. In fact, some of 'em was generals. I thank his papa was a colonel. Maybe that's why he was late. Just didn't want to help yah bring in Dillard."

Bass thought for a moment, and then said, "I sure didn't know that. Interestin' information, but I kind of doubt it 'cause there is a big reward for Dillard, and you know Heck likes to collect the money. In fact, that seems to be his main reason for bein' a marshal."

"It's possible I'm wrong," Cliff said. "But it sure might be the reason for 'im bein' late, or he just may have wanted Dillard to get away so he wouldn't have to share the reward."

"Whatever the reason, I'll just take it that he was late," Bass said. "You know, things happen like they is supposed to happen. Maybe if he'd been there, this day wouldn't have come."

"Guess you're right about that," Cliff said.

The men went back to listening to the rhythm of the train, and Bass began to wonder if his hunch was right. If it wasn't, they were wasting valuable time.

He consoled himself with the fact that at least the trip had given him and Cliff some time out of the saddle, and, for the first time, he was covering territory in the shade and with a cooling breeze.

As the train followed a bend in the tracks, Cliff stood and looked through the slats.

"We're 'bout to cross the river, and nothin' unusual has happened. But the sight of that fast movin' water sure is comfortin' to me. In fact, it sure reminds me of how coolin' swims used to be."

As the train started across the bridge, the sound of the whistle shattered the calm, and they felt the sudden clamp of the brake, followed by a slamming noise as the wheels screeched and the cars banged together as the slack came out of the couplings joining them.

As the train came to a grinding halt, the screeching whistle continued, sending the engineer's warning that he was being forced to make the stop.

Bass and Cliff jumped to their feet and rushed to the cattle car door. They pulled it open, only to face an upsetting sight. They were in the middle of the bridge, and their plan of jumping their horses out and giving pursuit was now in shambles.

It was thirty feet to the river, and the bridge was so narrow that all they could see were the ends of the railroad ties. It was impossible to get the horses out.

"Damn it!" Bass said. "We can't let 'em rob the train while we're stuck here. Cliff, can you see 'em through the slats?"

Cliff rushed to the front corner of the car. "I can see part of 'em. Looks like there must be at least five, maybe more."

"Can you get a shot at them from here?" Bass asked, quickly forming a plan.

"Not a clear one, and only if they stay back from the train. If they get closer to the train, I won't be able to see anything."

"You stay with the horses and let me get down and run down the

Two fisted justice

tracks," Bass said. "Give me a minute, and then get up on top of the car and unload on 'em. I don't care if you hit 'em. Just give 'em somethin' to keep 'em busy. I'll go down and try to get a clearer shot at 'em, and when we get 'em scattered, use my spyglass and see if you can see where Dillard goes. I'll try to get the track cleared and pull the train up so we can get the horses out. When I do, jump yours and Blaze out, and come and pick me up. I'm sure not goin' to let them bastards get away if I can help it."

  Bass jumped onto the narrow trellis and moved along the side of the car until he could get to solid ground. He broke into a run as soon as he was able and started to try and find an appropriate place where he could get between the cars.

  While he was doing this, Cliff began sending blistering fire from his Henry, immediately drawing returning fire from some of the robbers while others in the group were trying to pry open the mail car door.

  Cliff had been effective in that Bass could see two bandits sprawled on the ground. Bass rounded the corner of the railcar and, with his Winchester on his hip, started to fire in the direction of the thieves.

  His initial shock was at the number in the gang. There were still five on horseback with another two working at the mail car door.

  Bass' repeated shots took the group by surprise, but they immediately returned fire in his direction, forcing him back behind the car. While he was taking cover, the two at the mail car door mounted and another rider left the engine. They quickly joined the rest of the gang, and all turned their pistols toward Bass.

  The firing from the gang was intense as they rode away, and it forced Bass to stay behind his cover. When the men were several hundred yards from the track, they stopped firing and put their mounts in full speed.

  Bass stepped from his protected position and tried to locate Dillard in the bunch. Not being able to do this, he picked one rider and sighted in. By this time, they were at least five hundred yards from Bass, but he allowed for the wind and distance and squeezed the trigger.

  Bass thought he had missed his target, but in a few seconds his chosen target slumped in his saddle as his horse's pace slowed. The man swayed back and forth, all the while grabbing his shoulder. Finally, the rider kicked his horse and slowly turned him into the nearby trees.

  Bass rushed to the front of the train and quickly began removing the logs, railroad ties and brush the robbers had placed there. He soon was joined by members of the crew, and, with their help, the track was promptly cleared.

  Bass shouted, "Get the train movin' now! You got the horses trapped, and if we don't get movin', the bastards are gonna get away!"

The engineer pushed the throttle forward, and the drive wheels spun in response. The shrill screeching of the wheels and the powerful roar of the engine were followed by a great hiss and a cloud of steam. In seconds, the train lurched forward.

Bass hollered up at the engineer as the train went by, "Keep it goin'. We'll handle it from here." The lawman then turned and began running toward the cattle car. He could see the car's open door, and, in seconds, he saw Blaze in midair, then landing on the ground. The horse momentarily stumbled for footing but managed to gain his balance. Almost as quickly, Cliff and his mount cleared the opening with Cliff already in the saddle.

Bass stopped and quickly reloaded his rifle, knowing Cliff would soon be by his side with Blaze in tow.

"Did you see where they was headin'?" Bass asked Cliff, at the same time rushing to mount Blaze.

"Yep, got a pretty good idea. I think they split up just before they hit them trees," Cliff said.

"Could you see where Dillard went?"

"I feel sure he went to the left, and most of the others turned south."

"Let's forget about the others," Bass said. "We want Dillard. You lead, and I'll follow. When we get to the trees, I'll see if I can pick up his tracks."

Chapter 2

The Silent Storm

Bass soon picked up the track of the lone rider. He turned to look at the sun to see how much time they had to get their man.

That's when he saw to the southwest the most menacing cloud formation he could recall. It was moving rapidly and was black as midnight. The cloud showed rain falling from it and tremendous flashes of lightning dancing from the heavens to the ground. It seemed that there was no moment that some part of the heavens was not set ablaze with a display of galloping light. Within seconds of this display, the men began to hear the roar of thunder, seconds later experiencing thunder so violent that the ground shook and the trees quivered as the storm advanced at an incredible speed.

"My God, what in the world is goin' on?" Cliff asked, turning in his saddle to look with astonishment at the raging storm.

"Looks and sounds like a war is comin' for us. I ain't seen or heard nothin' like that since Pea Ridge," Bass said.

Bass stared for a moment before saying, "If we got any hope of catchin' Dillard, we best hightail it now. If that has as much rain in it as it looks, his tracks will be gone nearly as fast as that lightnin' is movin'."

Bass jumped into the saddle and put Blaze in full stride. The tracks were easy to read. There was one horse, and the ground was soft. As they started to get higher into the timber, the ground became less supportive of the imprints. Bass had to slow his pace, but he was relieved to see that the stride of the horse he was chasing had shortened to a slow gallop.

As they ascended the hillside, the new threat started to make its appearance. Suddenly the warm day seemed to turn to winter. A strong wind came rushing, bringing an incredibly fast drop in temperature. The first blast of wind made both men fight to keep on their hats, and the chill it brought caused them to turn up their collars. They were deluged with green leaves dislodged from the trees and an abundance of dust, dirt and small particles that were being hurled by the force of the wind.

Within seconds of the wind, ice cold rain started to fall in nearly a horizontal direction. The rain quickly was displaced by pellets of ice, so big that they inflicted pain as they struck the riders.

Bass shouted to Cliff, "We best get to that ridge and hope we can find some cover or this could be real bad."

They left the trail, now being pelted by ice that started to look like and feel like stones being thrown from heaven. Both riders hunched over in their saddles, holding on tightly as the wind and sleet punished them.

When they reached the ridge, they scurried around its base to its north side, providing them some protection from the wind while lessening the force of the sleet. Continuing to skirt the ridge, they came to an overhang that provided them the shelter that they had been seeking.

They immediately dismounted and pulled their slickers from their saddlebags. Removing their wet shirts, they quickly put on the slickers and backed up against the protective wall.

The men looked at the other and shook their heads as they tried to slap the moisture from their hats and squeeze the water from their soaked pants. It was startling how their bodies were now shivering when only moments earlier they had been suffering from the heat.

The thunder was still deafening and the lightning was closer than ever. It lit up the area as brightly as the photographer's flash when he had taken pictures of the U.S. Marshals at Fort Smith. The difference was that there seemed to be little if any break between flashes. The explosive roar of the thunder was never ending, making even their rock shelter tremble.

The men pulled their horses in close, using their wet shirt to cover the eyes of their mounts. The men hoped to lessen the horses' fear by shielding them from the illuminating flashes. While the action seemed to lessen the tension of the horses, the animals still were shivering and showing signs of great uneasiness. Bass pulled Blaze close and started whispering in his ear and stroking him. He continued to do so until the storm lessened.

As quickly as the storm started it subsided. While rumbling thunder could still be heard to the north of them, the rain, hail and wind quit.

Bass secured a clean, dry shirt from his saddlebag and pulled his Winchester from the boot. He hurriedly dried it and replaced it. Then he pulled his pistols and did the same with them.

While he was doing this, he turned to Cliff, who had been busy with his own horse and efforts to get dry. "Of all the damned luck," Bass said. "I'm beginnin' to think that Dillard is livin' a charmed life. Every time I get close to 'im, somethin' interferes."

"Well, I think we should just feel lucky that we got out of that with our skins. At least we're alive, and we'll find 'im when it's the right time."

"Now you're startin' to talk like me," Bass said. "I just hope there's another time. But I'm not through with this one. We're too close to stop now. Luck may come back to our side. So let's see if we can pick somethin' up. He had to take shelter same as us."

Bass mounted Blaze and patted him on the neck. He turned his head and started back around the ridge.

Cliff said, "You know, I think I'll go around the other way. It could double our chances of flushin' 'em out."

"Good idea. Go to it."

***

It was now nearly dark. Bass had changed his shirt, but his pants still were soaked and were starting to chill him.

He knew that if he was suffering, than Dillard must have the same problems. This drove him to keep on the hunt.

The ground was soaked, and on the uphill grade, it made the going slow and cautious, as Blaze stumbled and slipped trying to keep his footing. The air was clean and crisp, and Bass pulled it in. That's when he noticed the distinguishing smell of smoke.

Someone had a fire going, and there weren't but three people in the area. He knew that Cliff had no fire, so there was but one person who could be seeking warmth.

Again, Bass thought how lucky Dillard must be to find enough dry stuff to get a fire going. Bass just shook his head and thought, "Maybe it's not meant to be that I catch this man."

Bass turned toward the wind and dismounted. He pulled his Winchester from its boot and let his reins fall to the ground.

He stooped over and started heading in the direction from where the smoke had to be coming. He moved slowly and cautiously, knowing that if Dillard had a fire, the man was not thinking about running. He probably was sitting cozy and drying his clothes. Bass imagined how surprised Dillard would be to learn he still was being trailed.

By now, the sun was gone, and Bass' advance was complicated by the darkness, making it nearly impossible to find a place to step without breaking some of the newly fallen limbs that were the result of the storm, or to keep his footing in the mud on the hillside.

After several yards, he was rewarded with the sight of a fire just around the corner of a rock outcropping. He knelt and waited. In the same moment, the moon broke through the clouds to his back. He could not believe how big and bright it was after such a violent storm, at the same time feeling blessed that now he had some light to help with his approach.

Bass took a few more steps, then stood to see if he could observe what was happening near the fire.

Suddenly he felt a pain in his stomach, as if he had been kicked by a mule, and at the same time saw a flash and heard the report of a pistol as the wind left him and he fell forward. He had not felt such a pain since he was lashed years before with a black snake whip. He struggled to get his breath, and then lay still.

Bass was expecting to feel blood running from his stomach, but lying in the mud, he only felt the discomfort of the cold wet ground. He realized, though, that his face was in the mud, and his rifle was not in his hand.

He slowly turned his head to see if he could locate his rifle, but the moon was not helping, as it had gone behind a cloud, making it impossible to locate the firearm. Bass slowly worked his right hand down his side, reaching for his right Colt. It was not there. In fact his holster was not there. He then reached with his left hand for his left Colt and found the same emptiness.

The pain in his stomach subsided, and he started breathing better, but he was confused as to what had happened to his pistols.

A laugh brought him back to his senses. He could hear Dillard laughing in delight at Bass' prone body.

During this laughter, Bass heard Dillard slip and grasp a tree for support, followed by a string of cusses. During this sequence of events, Bass looked one more time for where he hoped the Winchester was. To his relief, it was there. He rapidly grabbed for it and turned his mud caked face toward where he had heard Dillard slip and stumble. Still in a prone position, Bass pulled the trigger of the Winchester. The projectile hit dead center in Dillard's body, silhouetted by the campfire that was to his back. Dillard crumpled in his tracks, pitching backward.

Bass immediately turned on his side and chambered another round. Now secure with the thought that he was armed, he began trying to figure out what had taken place.

The pain in his stomach was nearly gone, so he struggled to his feet. He felt his hips and found that it had not been a dream — his pistols were gone. With the aid of the returning moonlight, he searched the ground around him and found them lying nearby.

When he picked them up and tried to return them to their proper places, he found there was no longer a buckle on the gun belt. He then lifted his mud soaked shirt and saw that he had not been shot. His buckle had deflected the pistol shot before being torn away from his body.

Bass slowly gathered himself and walked toward the outstretched body of Bob Dillard. Before he reached it, Cliff came rushing up.

"Bass, are you awright? I heard the shootin' and got here as soon as I could locate you."

"Well, I guess I'm alright, but I came as close to getting' it as I ever have. Look here! The bastard shot my buckle off of my gun belt," Bass said, holding up his shirt.

"My God, that was close. I never seen nothin' like that."

"Yeah, and when Dillard's luck ran out on him, it did it in a big way," Bass said, obviously excited by the immediate events. "He got my belt buckle and not me. Then he slipped when he was coming to finish me, and he was outlined by his own campfire, so I was able to find him in the dark. I guess it goes to show you that when your time is runnin' out, no matter what advantage you got, it ain't gonna help.

"Before this all happened, I'd made up my mind that he had some kind of magic about 'im, and that I never was gonna get 'im. But when it was all said and done, he had no more luck than any of the varmints that I've tracked. And if you really want to know, I feel like I've all the luck a man could have. Well, on second thought, it ain't luck. The good Lord is just keepin' me around for somethin', and my mama will sure be proud that he seems to still be on my side."

Cliff said, "There's little doubt that you sure got somethin' lookin' after yah, 'cause by all rights, you shoulda not made this one out alive, and I sure would a hated to be the one that brought you back slung over a saddle."

"Well, thankfully you don't have to do that," Bass said. A broad smile covered his mud-encrusted face. "Now you given any thought what you was gonna do with your share of the reward money?"

They both broke into laughter.

Chapter 3

Sixkiller

It was late December, and it had been a good year for Bass. His accomplishments on the trail had paid well, and his family had kept production at the farm in a profitable manner.

Bass decided to take some time off and go home. He stopped by the telegraph station and asked the operator to send a message home telling his family that he was on his way. He knew that this would give them time to work out any problems they had, because the children did not like to have him involved in any discipline.

As he was waiting for the people ahead of him in line, he heard two local men talking and expressing their anger.

"It is a dirty shame what has come of this land. We gotta get things under control here. I was at a meeting the other day in Muskogee, and they continually talked of Statehood, but we all know that that ain't gonna happen with all these problems. Things like this is jest the thing they was talking about."

The other man said, "Yep, and he was such a nice feller. He's gonna be missed."

The two turned and saw Bass listening to their conversation. One of the men said to Bass, "Guess it really was bad news for you, marshal. I hear you was pretty close with 'im."

"What are you talkin' 'bout?" Bass asked. "I just got in, been on the road for several days and ain't heard no news."

"Well, I'm sorry to be the one that brings you the bad news then. Really sorry. It jest came over the telegraph that Sam Sixkiller got killed yesterday in Muskogee."

"My God, you sure of that?" Bass said, feeling something close to a punch in his gut.

"I know it's hard to believe, but that is what the news is. I sure hate to have to be the one that told yah."

Bass stood for a moment and looked at the man, then glanced at the floor. His mind raced. He could remember the first time he met Sixkiller. It was in Tahlequah when he and Sam had been the closest competition in the shooting contest, competitors and good friends. Of course, the thing that stood out most in Bass' mind was how Sam and his men had eliminated three of the bastards who had been involved in the killing of Bass' girlfriend, Jane.

Bass turned his back on the men and kicked the ground with his boot. He then looked up at the heavens and shook his head. His mind wondered back to Sam and how many times they had crossed paths.

Sam was the one who had given him the great introduction to Sheriff Donovan in Van Buren. That had brought about Bass purchasing the farm and the many jobs he had performed, tracking the Territory in search of fugitives with all the lawmen that Donovan had sent his way.

It was Sam who had taken him to the gunsmith where he had sold the magnificent shotgun and pistol he had taken off of English Bob. This money had played a great part in his purchase of his farm.

Damn, the more he thought about it, the more he realized what a great part Sam Sixkiller had played in his life.

Bass suddenly had a feeling of great loss. He found a bench and sat down. Unable to look up, he kept his eyes down while continuing to recall events were Sam had played a key part in his life.

In silence, he could not help but remember how his good friend Ben Horsechief had talked of the great influence that Sam had had on his life. Sam not only was Horsechief's uncle, but had been a father figure to him. Bass knew that his feeling of loss was nothing compared to what Ben must be feeling at this time. Ben had talked so much of his uncle and mentor — it was like he worshipped him.

Bass finally looked up, only to see the two men watching him. "Do you know when the funeral will be held?" he asked.

"No, but I'll bet the telegraph operator knows. The lines has been hummin' all day with the story," one of the men volunteered.

Bass was a man who always exhibited patience and courtesy, but he suddenly had a great urge to push his way to the front of the line and get his answer.

He didn't have to wait. The customer at the front of the line was Skinny Jonas, a Creek who Bass had known for years.

When Skinny finished paying for his message, he turned, walked to Bass and stuck out his hand.

"I am sorry for your loss," Skinny said. "I know how you and Sam were such good friends. It has to hurt, but you got to know that he is goin' to a good place."

"Skinny, do you know when the service will be?"

"Yeah, I am goin'. It will be at the Methodist Church in Muskogee tomorrow at eleven. There's a bunch of us that is goin'. In fact, there will be elders from all the tribes there. You know Sam was a great service to all of the tribes, and we all feel a great loss. It ain't right that a man like him gets gunned down, especially since he was unarmed."

"You mean that he was bushwhacked without bein' in a fight?" Bass asked, his voice rising.

"From what I hear, he was just goin' to the store for medicine or somethin', and these two just walked up and shot him dead. Sure ain't no way for a man like him to go, but you bein' a lawman know that it can happen any minute and any way."

"Sure do, but you never want to believe it could really happen. I best get goin'. I got some things to do before I hit the road," Bass said, rising from the bench. "Thanks for the information. I'll see you tomorrow at the church."

Bass turned and walked outside the railroad station. His stomach still was tight as he mounted Blaze and turned the animal toward the center of town. The chill in the December air only added to his feeling of emptiness.

Bass pulled up in front of the Hadley's General Store and dismounted. As he was tying Blaze to the rail, he noticed two freedmen that he often had problems with. They were standing and laughing on the porch. Bass quickly ascertained that they were discussing the death of Sam and taking great delight in the event.

Bass, for the first time in his life, had the urge to draw on them and put them out of their misery. He then realized that not everybody was feeling the loss like he was. He realized that there were many that would rejoice in the fact that Sixkiller had been eliminated. Sam had been a thorn in the side of those who spent their lives in lawlessness, and men like these were feeling relief with his absence.

As Bass got closer, they dropped their heads and turned to walk away. Before they had gone far, one turned and said, "Well, Bass, seems that there is one less of you bastards that is hasselin' us good people. Maybe, if'n we is lucky, yah is next." Then he turned as he and his companion hurried down the street.

Bass, shrugged his shoulders and started to reply, but decided it was better to go about his business. He picked up some supplies, which included ammunition for his rifle and pistol, and hurried back to Blaze.

He needed to get on the road. He wanted to get to Muskogee and find out the whole story, and he knew that Ben Horsechief would need some consoling at this moment.

Chapter 4

Lookin' for Justice

The first place Bass went in Muskogee was the funeral home. He knew that he would find people there who he could share thoughts with and find out the real story.

As he approached, he saw Sam's wife, Fannie, and her children leaving. She was accompanied by friends and relatives who supported her arms as she made her way. H e saw Ben holding her on one side.

As Bass reached them, he took off his hat, placed it over his heart and said, "I know there ain't much I can say, but I want all of you to know that I feel a great loss, and if there is anything I can do, please let me know."

Ben stepped from the assemblage and extended his hand. His eyes were red, and his faced was flushed.

When Bass reached for his hand, Ben pulled him close and embraced him with great feeling. He sobbed and patted Bass on the back for a few moments, then pulled himself away. His composure returned and his eyes narrowed.

"Bass, I'm so glad you're here. You said you are here to help, and the only thing I want from you is to help bring Sam's murderers to justice. We've got to get poor Sam in the ground, but as soon as that's done, I want you to come with me and find the bastards that brought this miserable day about."

"I told you I was here for you. If that is what will make you feel better, that is what I'll do," Bass promised, looking at Ben, then at Fannie.

Ben turned to Fannie, taking her hand. "You go on ahead. Let me stay here and talk to Bass some, and we'll join you later."

The men stood in silence and watched as the family left. Then Bass turned to Ben and said, "Now tell me. Who is we looking for, and what happened?"

"Bass, Dick Vann and Alf Cunningham was drunk and raisin' hell at the races here in town, and they just went crazy," Horsechief said. "They stole a shotgun and took a pistol off of a deputy and went on down the street and found Sam walkin' into the store to get some medicine. Then they just walked up on him and started this mess.

"I'm told that Sam pushed the shotgun away, but Vann just started pumpin' lead into him. Shot him four times, and when he was down on his hands and knees, they put one in his head.

"They left 'im dyin' in the street and skipped town. Cold-blooded bastards seemed to be enjoyin' every minute of it. Bass, Sam didn't even have a gun. He hadn't been feelin' well and was just tryin' to get his medicine."

At this point Ben choked up and tears came to his eyes. It was impossible to tell by his expression whether he was mourning the loss or releasing his pent up anger.

Bass stood for a minute and said, "I know both of 'em. Had a bad run-in with Cunningham a while back and thought he was in jail. I know he was a no-good, but wouldn't have thought he would a done nothn' like this."

"Well, he did. Had several witnesses that swear this is the way it happened, and I ain't restin' till they pay for it. My uncles Martin and Luke are hittin' the trail as soon as the funeral is over. Can you go with us?"

"Where they goin'?" Bass asked.

"Last time Vann got in trouble, he headed for Goose Creek Bend and got away clean. There has already been a posse lookin' there, but they ain't found nothin' yet."

"I know the area real good, snaked several people out a there," Bass said. "You can be sure that I'm with you. However, let's let Martin and Luke do their search, and you and I will use a different approach. I got a feelin' I know where they'll be, so we can scout some of the area I doubt that they know about."

"Bass I know you want 'em nearly as bad as I do, so I'll let you lead. I just want it done, and the sooner the better."

***

The funeral was a great testament to the long-serving lawman, and the amount of people in attendance was a suiting honor for a man who had served so long and well the people of the Five Tribes.

Bass was not sure, but it looked like there were more than a thousand people in attendance. He recognized many from different towns in the area, even some people from Arkansas. He was impressed with the reverence and admiration that the people showed this great man.

Something that really impressed him was how so many Indians from so many different tribes had gathered to pay their respects. Bass could not remember a time when he had witnessed so many tribal leaders gathered in one place.

Bass made sure Fannie knew he was there. As he shook her hand, she looked him in the eye and quietly said, "Bass, please help find the men who did this."

The sight of her in a black dress, children at her side, made a deep impression. It was so heartrending that for a moment he could not speak.

He patted her on the shoulder and said, "It'll be done."

***

After they had placed Sam in the ground, all those to be involved in the hunt met at the general store. Some needed ammunition, and some needed supplies. All, including the Sixkiller brothers and other family, wanted to be equipped for what might be a long time on the trail.

Ben introduced Martin and Luke to Bass. Both men looked at Bass approvingly.

"We have heard many great things of you from Sam and welcome you," Luke said. "Any help you can be is appreciated, and we know that Sam is glad you are here."

"There has been a reward of more than a thousand dollars put on these bastards, and we know that you will try your best to bring these lowlife murderers to justice," Martin added.

"Reward has nothin' to do with it," Bass said. "Sam was a good friend, and I'll do my best to help in any way. I understand that you fellers are goin' to Goose Creek Bend, and I think that's a good move, but I'm takin' Ben, and we're goin' a different direction. Some of us will come up with 'em, so don't worry."

The Sixkiller group soon mounted and went their way.

Bass said, "Come on, Ben. I've a contact about five miles out that could give us a lead on what is takin' place and cut time off this chase."

They headed toward the Young homestead and made good time.

When they arrived, Ed Young met them at the door.

Ed had been a friend of Bass' for years and often had helped with information about the lay of the land and the action in the area. He had been a Union solider who settled in the area, first working with the government in the Dawes office and later retiring to his homestead.

"Bass, how the hell did you know I was lookin' for some help? I got robbed last night and was fixin' to head to town to see if I could get some lawman to come out and give me a hand, and Lord, if you didn't just ride up."

"What happened, Ed?" Bass asked.

"After we went to bed last night I heard somethin' out at the barn and went to see what was goin' on. These two fellers jumped me and had the drop on me. They took me back to the house and took my two rifles and all my ammunition, as well as took all the food we had, and stole my horse. They popped me on my head is why I ain't left already. I'm not feelin' too fine at the moment. On top of that, I was gonna have to walk."

"Did you know 'em?" Bass asked.

"Knew one of 'em. He was that Vann guy. I'd seen him several times in town, and he was raisin' such a ruckus that I remembered him as someone I sure wanted to stay clear of."

"That's the guy we're lookin' for. Seems like we is on the right trail," Bass said.

Ed said, "Well, they now has a lot of firepower, so if you run into 'im and his partner, you'd better be careful."

"Ed, you should feel lucky that all you got was a knot on your head. Those two guys killed Sam Sixkiller, and we're on their trail."

"Lordy, they killed Sixkiller? That's terrible. Now I know why they were in such a state of fuss."

"I'm sorry for your trouble, and if we can get your stuff back, we will see that you get it," Bass promised.

"Bass, I know you will, and let me add, that I sure am sorry for the news. I know you was a friend of 'is."

"I got a bad feelin' for my loss, but this here is Ben Horsechief, and he is Sam's nephew," Bass said, regretting not making an introduction sooner.

Ed, stuck out his hand and said, "Sorry for meetin' you like this, and let me tell you that we are all gonna miss 'im."

Ben nodded and said, "Thanks we all are."

Bass turned to Ben and said, "We had better get a goin'. Your uncles may be gettin' ready to need some help."

***

The five miles was made in record time since it appeared the Sixkiller posse was in danger of running into more firepower than they were prepared to handle, and the thought of losing one more to these murderers was more than either Ben or Bass wanted to think about.

As they approached Goose Creek Bend, Bass sharply turned and headed toward the south end of the area. He knew that the posse probably had come in from the west. If his judgment was right they would either catch the killers in a holding position or flush out the desperados.

The two closed in on the wooded area that bordered the bend and Bass turned his horse toward a high ridge that bordered the river.

"That is the place where I think they is a layin' for, whatever comes after 'em. It gives 'em the high ground and good cover. Let's circle 'round. I know where there is a spot that will give us a perfect view of whatever is happenin' there."

Ben fell in behind and let the man with the experience lead the way.

They had not gone more than a quarter of a mile when the afternoon quiet was abruptly shattered by the sound of gunfire.

"They've made contact, just like I thought, they have the high ground on your uncles," Bass said.

The gunfire continued as the two men advanced. It sounded as if both sides were throwing lead, hopefully, the varmints were poor shots.

Bass dismounted and pulled his Winchester from the boot, Ben followed suit.

They worked their way through the overgrowth until the ridge became clear. From their position Ben and Bass could see that the pursued were defiantly in control of the hostility. With a clear view of the posse, the murders were raining intense fire on the Sixkiller posse. The high ground and the perfect rock fortress had made the men below easy targets, with little chance of relief.

Bass pulled Ben to his side and said, "From here, if you wait until they rise up from behind the rocks, you can get a clear shot at 'em. It's your choice, you can make it so hot for 'em that they give up, or you can take 'em down."

Ben thought for a moment and said' "If I wait, they may get lucky and hit one of the posse. Worse yet, they may get another one of my uncles. If they give up, they'll have made a choice. They never let Sam have a choice, so why should I?"

With those words, he steadied his rifle against a tree and waited. Alf was the first to reveal himself, and Ben squeezed the trigger. In a flash, the rifle fell from Alf's hands, and he pitched backward.

In a moment, Dick stuck his head over the edge of the boulder and shouted, "Hey, down there. I want a talk!"

Those were the last words he ever spoke. Ben's aim was on target with the area around Dick's head showing an instantaneous red glow as the man fell back. In less than thirty seconds, Ben had avenged his uncle's death.

Bass turned to him, as Ben was putting another round in his Winchester, and said, "You did good. I couldn't have done better. I think you made the right choice. Now I'll be leavin'. I feel that you've done what I would've done, and I'm sure Sam is proud of you. If anyone asks, tell 'em I was here and had to go. If they want to give me any of the reward money, tell 'em that my share goes to Fannie and the children."

Ben reached out his hand and grasped Bass's. "I want to thank you for your help, and I hope all the others do the same with the reward. The family is gonna need it."

"I just wish that this hadn't happened. Sam was a great man, and the Territory will greatly miss him," Bass said.

Chapter 5

Pete's Day

Pete came into the staging station and said, "Well, Bass, I'm ready, and it looks like Ed and Newly are itchin' to hit the trail. I see you have a lot of warrants, and it should make us a fist full of dollars. I have sure missed our runs together. It seems like they always have us going in different directions."

Bass nodded, letting the man continue. He knew that he did not have to answer Pete, because Pete could have a conversation with himself for days.

"I sure hated to hear about Sixkiller, Pete said. He was one hell of a man and it'll take someone special to replace him. As a matter of fact, I don't think he can be replaced. He always was most obligin' to me, and we sure put a lot of fellers in the jail with his help."

Bass shook his head and said, "I think you're right. No one will fill his boots. He just had the kind of way about 'im that made you respect 'im," Bass said. "But I know that his murderers won't be botherin' anybody again."

Pete responded, "We've lost way too many good men. It is up to us to make as miserable as possible the lives of those who think they can do as they please."

"Well, maybe we can get some of the bad ones out of the land on this trip. I know that it is sure good to have the old bunch back together. It really is, I even brought Dog along. He sure don't like stayin' in town, and I felt bad that I had to leave him there for a while," Bass said.

"Newly's been helpin' me study the warrants, and he says there are several with rewards, but none are big," Bass said, "I think I got most of 'ems names down, but we have a long trip, and I should be able to get a better fix on 'em as we make our rounds."

The morning was brisk, and the trail was familiar, so the advancement to the usual first night's camp went well.

Dog lay on the wagon, keeping his usual watchful eye on the trail. From time to time, he would raise his head, perk up his ears and peer into the woods. He knew that there were rabbits and squirrels in abundance and was just biding his time about when to strike.

When they rounded a bend in the road the opportunity presented itself. There was a rabbit at least one hundred yards from cover, and Dog bolted from the wagon seat as if he had been shot out of a gun.

In short order he chased the rabbit down and made the first capture of the journey. The canine appeared proud that he hadn't lost his hunting skills, as he returned to the wagon.

"Well, if Dog's luck is anything like ours, we should have a right nice month, "said Pete.

"We sure have had plenty of luck in the past, so I see no reason this trip shouldn't go good. The thing is, that it seems that no matter how many we bring in, they just keep makin' more of 'em. Good for our business, but sure is a problem for the good people here," Bass said.

***

The camp was set up in its usual place, and the men settled down for a good night's rest. This could be one of the few, as there were many miles to cover, and so many of their captures were made at night. By now, Bass and the crew had grown so accustomed to theior night-time work that it was taken as a matter of fact.

In the glow of the welcomed fire, their talk turned to family. Ed asked Bass how things were at the home place. "The kids are doin' well in school, and my hired men keep the gardenin' and horses goin' right good. I really miss time at home, but my real likes are here on the trail. It just seems that there is no place where I can continually test my skills, and the thrill of the hunt is just fulfillin'.

"One of the things that Jennie has got me into is the church. I go every Sunday when I'm home, and durin' the week, I go over and help 'em build their new buildin'. I find that it is quite contentin'," Bass continued.
"I has worked so hard that they has made me a deacon. My preacher is so proud to have me there, and he tells me that I am doin' the work of the Lord. He says that God has chosen me to carry a mighty sword to help those that can't."

Pete said, "I feel the same way 'bout the trail. I hope yah preacher is right. I know my pa was a God-fearin' man, and, of course, the thing that drives me is hopin' someday I will run onto the bastards that kilt him. I think I will probably hang up my badge when that is accomplished, maybe find me a lady and settle down. Might even find time to go to church, It'd sure be a change. I've been in the saddle since I was knee-high to a toad frog, and I'm not sure I could make the change, but it might be fun to try."

Bass and the others nodded in a sign of understanding. Then Bass steered the conversation back to the matter at hand,"In the mornin', let's head up to Muskogee and Tahlequah. I got a feellin' that there'll be some good huntin' there."

"Bass,yah is the boss. I'm just along for the ride, and, of course, a little action."Pete said.

***

The next morning the three left Newly and Dog and started the trip north. They had not gone far when they came across a Cherokee on his pony, with his wife walking behind.

Bass greeted him in Cherokee and asked if he had seen anything suspicious.

The Indian pulled his pony to a halt and said, "There's a group of fellers camped up the trail a piece that has a string of horses that sure don't look right. I have several friends that have lost horses in the past few days, and I know that at least one of the horses in the bunch looks like my friend's. They are white guys, or I would have already headed to the Light Horse, but I knew that it would be a waste of time."

"Where did you see 'em last?" Bass asked.

"'Bout two miles up the trail and then off to the east, campin' on the creek. They didn't seem in no big hurry. They was eatin' breakfast when I went by."

"Where does your friend live that lost the horse and does it have a brand?" Bass inquired.

"His place is up by Tahlequah, and his name is John Lightfeather. Anybody up that way can tell you where he lives."

The Indian then drew a likeness of a snake in the dirt, say that his friends horse would have a brand on his right front shoulder that resembled the drawning.

"Thanks for the information. Sounds like you might get credit for gettin' your friend's horse back."

As they parted, Ed asked, "Why was the woman walkin' and the man riding?"

Bass turned to him and said, "I guess she didn't have a horse."The three lawmen hurried up the trail. When they got near the location given by the informant, they stopped and listened.

They could hear laughter and voices coming from the creek. The men dismounted, spread out and quietly advanced through the woods, entering the encampment. The men entered the area from different directions. This caught the four suspects completely by surprise. Before they realized what was happening, Bass said, "I'm Bass Reeves, U.S.Marshal, and I'd like to have a look at your horses."

The four looked at each other, and for a moment, it looked as though they were going for their pistols. The fact that Pete had his pistol pointed toward them, before they could make a move quickly changed their minds.

Pete said, "Just to make us all a little more comfortable, why don't yah undo your belts and let 'em shootin' irons fall to the ground."

The four did as instructed, and Bass walked into the tied-out horses. In short order, he located the horse described by the Indian and returned to the four men at the campfire.

"Well, seems that you got a pretty good lookin' string there. It also seems like you got a lot of different brands in the bunch. You got any reason for that?"

One of the men said, "We been buyin' 'em here and there and was takin' 'em to Texas."

"Really?" Bass asked, "You got some paper, I guess?"

After a pause, one of the men said, "No, we was fordin' the river, and they got washed away."

"Then tell me the name of the man who sold you the horse with the snake on his right front shoulder from?"

"I don't remember." the man said.

"Tell you what, you fellers turn around and put your hands behind you, and we'll take you to see Judge Parker. He will give you some time to try to come up with the name."

***

After the men were secured, Bass said, "Ed, take 'em back to camp. We is gonna take the horses toward Tahlequah and see if we can find the owners. If not, we will leave 'em with the sheriff, and he can hold 'em 'til someone comes in and claims 'em. When you finish, come on up to Tahlequah and check with the sheriff. He'll tell you where to find us."

Pete and Bass took the string and headed toward Tahlequah. They passed several homesteads and stopped at each to see if any of them were missing horses or if they knew any horses in the group. The men were able to return several of them, to their grateful owners. They took the remaining to the Tahlequah sheriff's office.

While visiting with the sheriff, the lawman told Bass and Pete, "I know yah fellers are lookin' for trouble-makers, and I jest thought that I should tell yah that there were five fellers here a couple days ago that were jest spoilin' for trouble. I was fortunate that nothin' happened, but I know it'll only be a matter of time before they pull somethin' off."

"Did you get their names? I might have a warrant for some of 'em?" Bass said.

"One of 'em was a Hank Davis, and the only other name I got was a Ferber."

Peter instantly turned toward the sheriff and put full attention into what he was saying. He immediately said, with his eyes focused directly at him, "Sheriff, yah got any idea which way they went?"

"One of the girls over at Miss Kate's said they were goin' to Nowata, and that Hank Davis guy told her to be ready for him when he came back, 'cause he was gonna have a passel of money and wanted her full time."

"What was her name?" asked Bass

"They call her Millie, but I don't know what her real name is. Why?" Bass said, "Just like to know all I can know."

Pete had started showing signs of great anxiousness. He was pacing and more agitated than Bass had ever seen him.

"Pete, what's your problem?" Bass asked.

"The Ferber's are some of the ones I'm lookin' for. We gotta hit the trail. If for no other reason than they surely are plannin' on robbin' somethin'."

"Pete, take it easy. You don't have to sell me. I'll go with you now, and we'll see what we can come up with. I've some warrants to serve in Nowata anyways, so it's a just trip. Sheriff, when Ed gets here, tell 'im we're headed for Nowata, and he needs to go there. We'll find him in town if he don't find us first."

***

Pete and Bass headed for Nowata after they stopped at Mary's restaurant for something to eat. Bass had the cook fix some bread with a slab of beef and a jug of honey for the road. He knew they would not stop, once they headed out.

Pete was so uneasy that Bass had to keep holding him back. "You know we'll catch 'em, and we got plenty of time, too. You been lookin' for this guy for a long time. A few more days won't make no difference."

"That's just it, I been lookin' for a long time, and I'm itchin' to get it over with." Pete said.

"I promise you that you'll get your chance, if I have to track 'em to Kansas," Bass promised. "Now, if we catch 'em, let's take it slow and easy. If we play it right, you may be able to find the other ones."

The pair road directly to Nowata. Bass had some warrants he could have served on the way, but he knew that Pete was so focused on getting

Two fisted justice

Ferber in his sights that he did not want to waste any time. He could serve warrants on the way back.

Before they entered Nowata, Bass and Pete put their badges on the inside of their jackets. They had decided that if they got a chance, they would try to get as close to these trouble-makers as they could. It might prove interesting what they could learn, if they waited to make their play.

The streets were nearly empty when they entered town. It was still daylight, and the shops were open, but this was a Wednesday, and most of the action did not take place in town during the middle of the week. It would have been a different scene if it had been Saturday, when the streets buzzed with all the folks in the area buying and trading.

They slowly rode down the street, paying special attention to the horses tied in front of the saloons.

When they got to the third saloon, they noticed several horses that looked like they had been trailed hard in the past.

"Let's just pull up here and stroll in and have a look-see," Bass said. "If we don't find 'em, we can walk down to the other places, my legs could use a little stretching' 'bout now any ways."

As they entered the saloon, each took their hats off and slapped them against their legs. The dust flew from their hats and pants. They returned the hats to their heads and walked to the bar.

The barkeep knew Pete, as he walked toward the bar, Pete put his finger to the middle of his lips and winked at him. Then he said, "My good man, could yah get me and my friend a nice glass of cool beer? We is sure dry from the ride."

The bar-keep instantly understood. As he placed the beers in front of the pair, he turned a glancing eye and nodded his head toward the table in the far corner, where five men were talking in a low tone.

There was an empty table next to the five, and Bass and Pete slowly worked their way to the table. They sat down where Pete was facing the men while drinking his beer.

After a few moments, Pete said toward the table, "Hey ain't yah Hank Davis?"

One of the men instantly turned his head and said, "How'd ya know my name?"

"Yah is famous. I was over at Kate's place the other night. I had seen yah in there before, and Lady Millie could do nothin' but talk about you. She said yah was the greatest stud she had ever seen. If I was yah, I'd be tellin' the world about my abilities."

All of the men at the table started to laugh and slap the man on the shoulder. A grin and then a smile filled his face, and he said, "I been tellin' ya guys I was a stud, and now ya is hearin' it from a stranger. I guess yah can't keep a secret of bein' that good."

The men continued to laugh and point at Davis. He, of course, loved all the attention and joined the merriment.

Davis then asked, "Kid, what's yah name?"

Pete replied, "Yah just called it. They call me Kid Good Eye. Guess they did that cause one of 'em don't look right. The problem is that no one knows which'n is the good un. This here is my partner, in rough and dangerous deeds, Black Jim. We had three Jim's that rode with us. One was Tall Jim and one was Slim Jim. We had to have some way of tellin' 'em apart."

The table of men started to laugh even louder, and finally, one of them said, "Hey, can we buy yah fellers a beer?"

Pete said, "How about if I bought all of yah a bottle of whiskey? Black Jim don't drink that hard stuff, and I been hankerin' to find some fellers to share a bottle with."

"Sounds good to us, why don't yah come over to the table?"

Bass simply stared at the table and said, "If you don't mind I think I'll set here and nurse my beer. Then I'll go out and make sure that the horses get their oats. But the Kid can join you."

Pete motioned for the barkeep to bring a bottle, then scooted his chair into the gathering.

Bass left and took care of the horses, but knew that he should not stay long. He knew that a show was about to begin, and he had no desire to miss any of it.

When he returned, all of the men at the table were taking turns at the bottle, now more relaxed with the conversation.

Bass walked to the bar and stood where he could keep an eye on the group, in case he might be needed.

Pete was talking more and acting like the liquor was taking over his better senses.

He slowly and cautiously asked the names of the men. He was pleased when one said his name was Jake Ferber. He could hardly control himself when he learned that another was Luke Campsey.

From where Bass was standing, it was evident that Pete was having a hard time controlling himself, but to his credit, he settled back and just stared at the two before returning to his conversation.

After hearing their names, Pete said, "Say, I think I've heard of yah guys. Didn't yah ride with the Quantrill bunch durin' the war?"

"We all did. It was a great time, and we is jest sad that 'em days is over. Been hard gettin' along without the action. But we try to keep our hands in excitin' and profitable activity."

"I'll bet it was sure excitin'," Pete said. "I jest wish I'd been old enough to have joined yah.

He started to talk about what a great shot he was, and how he was one tough desperado. He told about holding up stagecoaches and robbing banks in Texas, and how he and Black Jim needed to find some action. The men, in their relaxed state, also told of recent exploits, and how they were planning a new, bigger job, that was going to need more men.

Pete showed approval for what they said and continued to talk of his exploits. The more he talked, the more great accomplishments he seemed to remember. His stories kept getting bigger and bolder, and he appeared to be getting more loosed tongued as the whiskey took hold.

The men were enjoying the presentation with great interest, and, finally, one of them said, "We has got a job comin' up that yah might fit in with, but all I've heard from yah is talk. I doubt that yah can beat me in a shoot off and I am willin' to bet yah ten dollars. On top of that,if you can beat me, we will let you join us. I get the feelin' yah is full of bull. I don't believe yah can even see out of 'em eyes, much less sling a pistol."

Pete looked at him and said, "I got ten dollars, and I got my Colts. Where do yah wanta do this?"

"Let's just step out in the back here and see what yah can do."

"Let's do it," Pete said. As they left out the back, Bass silently followed.

The men entered the alley, and one of the men walked about fifty feet from where Pete and his competitor were standing. The man placed a bottle on a rock.

Farber told Pete, "Why don't yah take the first shot?"

Pete drew his pistol and took careful aim. He squeezed the trigger, and a cloud of dust erupted about two feet in front of the bottle.

The men started to laugh. They were now sure that this desperado with so many tales was just a bag of wind.

Ferber pulled his pistol and instantly shattered the bottle.

"That's ten yah owe me."

Pete removed his spent cartage and replaced it, then said, "Why don't yah and Campsey here take these four bottles down there and place 'em were the other one was. I've somethin' that I think will impress yah, and I'll bet yah another ten."

The two laughed and said, "Where's the ten?"

Pete flipped a ten dollar gold piece at the two and said, "Now, if yah ain't afraid to take my challenge, get the bottles down there. I'm gonna show yah somethin' that will change your life, that is if yah ain't afraid."

The two chuckled as they walked to their destination. Once there,

Judge Parker & Bass Reeves

they placed the bottles in a row and turned to return.

Pete said, "Just stay there. I have somethin' to ask yah. Yah boys ever been to Kansas? While yah was there, do yah remember killin' a man with no weapon as he was walkin' from the outhouse back to his home and family? Just in case yah can't remember his name it was Eaton."

The two men stopped in their tracks and turned toward each other with a startled look on their faces. The response from both illustrated that they were starting to recall events from the past.

"I know the answer, and I'm tellin' yah that I'm that man's son, and I has been lookin' for yah for a long time."

Bass was standing behind the other three, who heard the sound of the cylinder turning as Bass cocked his pistol. At the same time, Bass said, "You boys just stand still. My friend has some business to do, and you need not think about gettin' involved."

Pete said, "My name is Frank Eaton, and I aim changin' the bet. What we is now doin' is called bet yah life. It's a fair gamble, you two against an old one-eyed boy. Cause I aim to put yah guys in the ground for what yah did. Now, when yah feel lucky, yah can reach for yah irons."

The two were now in deep thought. They stood and looked at their challenger for several seconds. They started to speak, then appeared to have made up their minds that they had seen their challenger shoot and didn't see a problem with this challenge. On top of that, they had faced many a man in their sordid lives and could see no problem taking on this cross-eyed, loud mouth.

While they were in thought, Pete said, "Well, yah yellow-bellied bastards, now that yah is facin' someone who might be able to fight back, yah kinda seem cowardly."

This was all the goading the pair needed. They both reached for their weapons. They were fast and smooth, but no match for Pete. He drew and fired both .45's just as they were clearing their holsters.

Pete's accuracy and speed was astounding. His shots were directly on target, and he hit both men in the center of their chests. Ferber had gotten his pistol out of his holster. As Pete had saved him for his left hand shot, the man's pistol discharge was in the dirt.

As the two were falling, Pete put another round in each of them. He stood with his pistols smoking and watched as the two men he had wanted to kill so badly crumpled to the ground.

Pete turned to Bass, and the three men he had covered. "Yah fellers are under arrest for the robbery of the Bartlesville Bank and the General Store at Big Cabin. Yah just confessed to it in there at the table. Before I take yah in, do yah know where the other Ferber is? If yah tell me, I might let yah go."

The three looked at each other, and one of them said, "If I knowed, I'd tell yah, but I did hear Ferber say that he had a brother livin' somewhere near Fort Gibson sometime back."

"By the time we get to see Judge Parker, yah might remember better, and I might do my part in testifying in your case. But I want yah to know that the judge takes a dim view of those that rode with Quantrill. So the more information yah come up with, the better it will be for yah."

Bass said, "I am gonna take you one at a time over to visit your friends for the last time, and the one that comes up with the best information for Pete will get my testimony in front of the judge. Those that don't will just have to hope the judge has some mercy for your miserable souls."

Bass walked each down the alley, and with their backs to the others, let them talk.

When he was finished, he called Pete to the side and said, "I think that the Fort Gibson lead is about all we can get, but I would like for you to stay on this road with me, and we'll circle by Fort Gibson on the return."

"Bass, I really want to go now. I've been carryin' this load for a long time, and I need to get it unloaded."

"I can sure understand that, but a few more weeks ain't gonna make much difference."

"Just can't do it. Yah got Ed, and yah said that the warrants weren't filled with anything that yah and he can't handle. So I guess I will be a goin'."

"Well, my friend, I understand. The best of luck to you, and may the hunt be to your likin'." Bass said.

Chapter 6

Younger's Bend

In a few days, Bass had assembled his crew and picked up a new batch of warrants. He had rested long enough and wanted to get back on the trail. There was work to be done and money to be made, so he saw no reason to stay idle.

Bass said, "Newly, this time out, let's alter our route and head west for a spell. We might jest run the trail backward jest to see if we come up with anything different."

"Sounds good to me. I was kind a getting' tired of stoppin' in the same old place, time and time again. In fact, some of them trees seem like they had grown a foot since we first stopped there."

When they got close to Younger's Bend Bass said, "Set up camp here. I'm goin' over by the river a little and see what I come up with."

This was Bass's second visit to Younger's Bend. His first had been just a social visit to see if the invitation that Belle had extended had any merit. It had proven to be just as she had promised, and he had fulfilled his promise not to bother her visitors unless she gave some type of approval.

They had visited about horses and her conflict with Judge Parker, and he had met a few of the travelers who seemed to be drawn to the comfort of the home, as well as the famous spring water.

Bass also felt that just the fact that some traveler might run into some famous or infamous passerby must have been a stimulus to draw all sorts of drop-ins. He also thought that they might have just altered their trip simply to see what a fine lady in the middle of this hostel country might be wearing.

Bass entered the little settlement and still was surprised at how nice and well kept the area was, but then he thought that it should be, it was run by a well schooled lady who prided herself in her education and Southern hospitality, in spite of the fact that she was equally viewed as a hell-raising law-breaker by many others.

Bass led Blaze to the spring and drew water. He went directly to the much talked about spring and again was impressed by its flavor and coolness. He emptied his canteen and refilled it from the spring. Then he led Blaze back to the hitching rail where there were two other horses. He made sure that his badge was now behind his jacket and entered the building.

Belle was standing near the door and smiled as he entered. She was dressed much differently this time. Her head was covered with a large grey hat that had a huge white plume waving in the air and she was wearing a flowing black dress. The one thing that had not changed was the pair of pearl-handled pistols strapped to her hips. She walked toward him as he approached and said, "I was wondering how long it would take you to get here. You have come at a slow time, but that will give you time to meet a few friends of mine."

She then leaned over close to him and said, "I have it on good advice that the three Jamison brothers are gonna be comin' by tonight, and I know they are wanted by Texas, if not other places. They are no friends of mine. They are low-life and sure give me no respect. I would be glad if you took them off of my hands."

"That's really interestin'," Bass said. "I have a warrant for three Jamisons right here in my pocket. Figger they is the same fellers."

She then turned to the two men at a table in the center of the room and said, "Doc would you and Idas mind if we joined you at the table. I'd like for you to meet a friend of mine."

Both men looked at Bass and seemed to pause. Then Doc said, "If he is a friend of yours we would be more than happy to have you join us. We might get some lies or some news that we haven't heard."

They went to the table, and Belle brought a new bottle of whiskey with her. As she sat it down she said, "Doc Jesse and Ides Willingham, this is Bass Reeves, a new friend of mine, I think."

Ides looked at him and said. "I know yah. We meet here last time you stopped, and I sent a message for you on the telegraph a while back, but I am gonna let Doc figure out who yah is."

Doc said, "Glad to meet you. Join in on the conversation. What do you do, Mr. Reeves?"

"I breed horses and collect people." Bass said.

Doc said, "I understand breedin' horses, but what do you mean you collect people? Are you some kind of preacher?"

"Well, it seems as though there are a number of people in the Territory that have lost their way. I don't preach to 'em. I take them back to Fort

Smith, and Judge Parker helps them change their direction."

Both men broke out laughing, and a big smile crossed Belle's face.

Doc said, "I know who you are now. I thought that I knew you when you came in, but I couldn't imagine that you would be in this place, and when Belle introduced you as a friend, I was really thrown off track."

Belle said, "You know me. I can see a spark of good in a man, I'll accept him until he proves me wrong. I have heard too many good things about this man to let his choice of occupation keep me from at least treating him with a little dignity."

Ides said, "Where yah got yah horses? I'm always lookin' for a good mount."

"I have a place just outside of Van Buren. Not a lot of horses, but I like to think that those I has are good ones."

Belle said, "You know, I got a gray filly from a man named Pickens that said he got her from a Negro man down by Van Buren."

Bass thought for a moment, and then asked, "Was your name Belle Reed then?"

"It sure was. I got a boy named Eddie Reed that will be in here in a little bit."

"Well, I was the man that sold Mr. Pickens that filly. How'd she do for you?"

Belle poured herself a half a glass of straight whiskey and drank about half of it with one swallow. As she set the glass down, a smile crossed her face. "Let me tell you about that filly.

"There was a guy in North Arkansas that had made a tub of money in the lumber business. He had this huge black stallion that he raced against anything. That horse was a runner and had not been beaten.

"I heard about him, and took my Indian jockey and Dorothy, that is what I call her, to his place, and challenged him to a race. I bet him five hundred dollars that Dorothy could outrun his stallion.

"He jumped at the challenge, and after a couple of days rest, we hooked 'em up. I knew in my heart that the stallion couldn't outrun Dorothy, but I told my jockey to never get ahead and to let the stallion win by at least two lengths.

"He followed my instructions and held Dorothy back until the last quarter of a mile. He then let her loose just enough to know that the next time all he had to do was let her go a little earlier.

"I paid the man and acted like it was the last five hundred I had. He showed me no sympathy, and that was just what I wanted.

"In about two months, I brought my jockey back with Dorothy, and I told the man that I had sold my ranch and would bet him five thousand dollars that his horse couldn't do it again.

"Just like before he jumped at the chance to take all the money that a poor lady had.

"This time I told my Jockey just to run fast enough to win. I sure didn't want the word to get out in all of Arkansas that I had a horse that could not be beat.

"My jockey did just what I told him, and he let the filly only win by about a head. Now you talk about someone that was crying. This man threw a wall-eyed fit. I thought he was going to kill his jockey, blamed it all on him. He finally paid the five thousand.

"I raced her for about three years, and she never got beat. As a matter of fact, there never was a horse that got close to her. She made me a pile of money.

"So, Bass, I just thought that I liked you. Now that I have put this all together, you are really an extra good friend of mine.

"To end the story,I still have Dorothy. She has had me seven fouls, and they all have been good horses, but none of them as good as she."

Bass smiled, "I knew she was a winner, and I'm glad you got 'er. You say you still have 'er. I would really like to see 'er."

"She is gone now, but we will arrange a time, or I might just ride her to Fort Smith and let you get a look at her."

Ides stood and said, "Well, I had best get on the road to Quinton. My girl friend, Winnie will be wonderin' what happened to me. Ihope I never need you marshal, but it is good to know yah is in the Territory."

Doc Jesse and Bass sat for a while, and Belle went to the back and brought her son, Eddie out to meet Bass.

There was something about the boy that Bass liked immediately, and before he parted. Bass said, "When you get old enough, come to Fort Smith, and we'll sign you up as a marshal."

Eddie looked at Bass for a moment and dropped his head. "You know my mother and the Judge don't get along. How would that be possible?"

"Let me tell you, I know that the two of 'em ain't friendly, but the Judge is a fair man, and he only judges people on what they can do, not on who or what they are. How do you think I got my job? So if you want to give it a try and you stay out of trouble, come on over. I'd be glad to work with you."

Eddie had a look in his eyes like he was contemplating the offer. He then said, "You know, that sounds like something I might be interested in. When I get a few more years on me, I might just come and see you. I got to go now and tend the horses, but I sure will keep that in mind."

Eddie stuck out his hand, and Bass firmly grasped it.

"I sure hope you give it some thought."

Belle had given Bass a tip, and he felt that this was the first test of their friendship. He would wait and see if the Jamisons showed up.

His wait was short. He heard horses approaching and the laughter of men as they approached the door.

Bass pulled his big black hat down over his eyes and waited to see what developed.

When the men entered, Bass sized them up, and then softly said to Doc Jesse, "You might ought to make your way to the door. It might get a little excitin' here in a minute, and I sure'd hate to lose a friend that I just made acquaintances with."

Doc Jesse sat for a short time and apparently was considering what his move should be.

The tall Jamison said, "Hey lady, give us a bottle, we is mighty thirsty."

Belle asked, "Do you intend on paying for this one? You know you walked out last time without paying. I don't mind sharing what I got, but for someone to not offer to repay me for my hospitality gets under my skin. Tell you what I will do. Pay me for the last bottle, and pay for this one, and we will be square."

"Damn bitch! You sure ain't actin' friendly," he snarled."

"Well, I am telling you the next time you call me bitch, you will learn just how unfriendly I can be. I run a business here, and I expect my customers to act like they have a little civility when they enter. If you don't want to do that, I don't need your business." Belle told him bluntly.

"Please excuse my brother," one of the other Jamisons said. "He ain't got much learnin' and always figures a woman that sells whisky don't need no respect."

"Well, he is sadly mistaken, and I would advise you to get his act cleaned up if any of you ever want to come in here again. I am a well-schooled and properly-raised lady, and I tolerate no disrespect, is that understood? Now give me my money or get the hell out of here."

The shortest Jamison placed the money for both bottles in her hand and said, "I'm sorry if there was any misunderstanding."

"Well, I want you to know that I don't tolerate smart mouths or cheap attitudes. I'm a lady first and foremost. I expect you to treat me with more respect and respect my house. I have little tolerance for ungentlemanly attitudes. Now, the less you say will probably be the better."

The brothers dropped their heads and stood in silence. They had not been talked to in such a manner in years, and it seemed to have caused them great discomfort. After a few moments of silence, they then proceeded to rapidly consume the contents and visit among themselves.

Two fisted justice

As the three men, were standing near the table on the other side of the room, started to get louder, Bass said, "Doc, it has been a pleasure visitin' with you, but you need to stand and go to the door, and on your way out, be sure and tell Miss Belle good night."

The Doc needed no more encouragement. He did exactly as Bass had suggested, except that he picked up the half full bottle of whiskey and tucked it under his arm, as he departed, Stopping long enough to tip his hat and wish Belle a good evening. He followed that with instructions that she put the bottle of whiskey on his bill. He surely did not want to anger her; his exposure to her wrath with the Jamison's was not what he cared to experience.

The room was gradually getting louder. They talked and laughed and became more boisterous as the contents of the bottle lowered.

Bass shouted above the noise, "Say, fellers. Can any of you read?"

The three turned toward him, and the shortest one said, "I can read readin' but I can't read writin'. Why?"

"Well, I got some readin' here that I sure could use some help with."

"Tell you what, why don't you go to school and get some learnin'?"

The three brothers broke into laughter, as each threw back a shot of whiskey.

Bass reached his left hand across his body,and pulled out his pistol and held it under the table, while his right hand covered the papers that lay on top of the table.

"Gentleman, I hate to stop your fun, but I think these papers is addressed to you."

The tallest one of the brothers asked, "What the hell do you mean, addressed to us?"

"Well, if I'm not mistaken, you is the Jamisons, and these here papers is warrants for your arrest. Seems you has been naughty, and it is time to go see the judge."

As all of the brothers turned toward Bass, their laughter stopped, and the smiles that had once covered their faces turned to questioning looks of disbelief.

The tall one said, "You is gonna set there by your lonesome and tell the three of us that you want us to come to jail with you?"

"No, I think you misunderstood me. Me and my friend want one of you to come over here and read this piece of paper and see if you need to come to jail with me."

"What friend?"

"The one that is pointed between your legs, friend."

"I doubt that."

"I'll tell you what, you can doubt it all you want, but the first one of you that makes a stupid move,I am gonna make a steer out of, and then the others will realize that it ain't no bluff."

After those words were spoken, like a troop of dancers, all of the men shifted their legs to protect their private area.

While they were making up their minds about what would be their next play, they heard the hammer of a pistol cock at their back.

Belle said, "Gentlemen I don't have a dog in this fight, but none of you are going to shoot up my place. I just got this mirror in from Saint Louis, and it cost more than any of you is worth. Earl, step over there and read the paper like the man asked. If it's not for you, I will cover you as you leave. If it is, lay all of your pistols on the table. Do it now. I am tired of all this messing around."

Earl stepped forward and looked at the papers. He read all three and said, "They is for us boys. I guess we had better do as the lady said."

Bass said, "Lift them pistols with your fingertips slowly. We is this close to a peaceful settlement. There ain't no need for bloodshed now."

The brothers did as instructed, and Bass rose and secured their hands behind them.

Bass turned to Belle and said, "I am sorry, lady, if I caused you any troubles, and I thank you for makin' this as easy as possible.

"Someday I'll drop back by, and I hope to see your horses."

When he headed through the door with his prisoners, he was shocked to see the Doc standing outside, where he had been witnessing the action.

As he passed, the Doc said, "Nice work, Bass. It was a pleasure to watch you work. I hope to see you again sometime."

***

They didn't get back to camp until after Newly and Ed were in bed, but Bass needed no assistance in fastening the men to the restraining chain because Dog kept a careful eye on each with a low growl and his fangs showing.

Chapter 7

Larry Keating

One more trip. One more hot day. Such were the summers in the Territory. While generally miserable, the thing that was always unknown was how hot it would be or if you would be caught in a torrent of rain.

This trip had been plagued with downpour after down-pour, making the usual search for lawbreakers that much harder, as well as the return trip much slower. It seemed that every creek and stream in the Territory was on a rampage and working to slow Bass and his group on their return to Fort Smith.

As they waited once again for the water to subside, there wasn't much for them to do but set in the shelter of the tents and visit about past exploits and adventures. In the middle of a conversation Bass, rose and wandered to the water's edge, hoping to see signs of relief from the rising waters that blocked their crossing.

He turned and observed that there were at least two more camps set up on the creek's bank, groups also waiting to cross. He noticed that some of the men milling around the sites gave the impression that they were more than average travelers. They just had that look that Bass had observed so many times, of men with some kind of trouble in their heart or skullduggery on their mind.

Bass returned to his dry secure camp and called for Newly to come outside. He wanted to be able to talk without the seven prisoners hearing what they were saying.

"Newly, why don't you take some coffee over to the camp over there and just offer it to the fellers there, as a friendly gesture, and strike up a conversation, if you can. See if you can find out any of their names. You know the warrants as well as me, and we might get lucky. This trip has been so unproductive and uncomfortable that maybe we might have some luck by havin' culprits just volunteerin' to join our party."

"Sounds like a right fine idea. I got the grub already done for the evenin', and I'm as bored as I can be."

Newly took some coffee from his store. He walked through the trees that had completely hidden the prison wagon from the view of anyone in the tents waiting on the creek's edge.

Newly had been around felons for so many years that he felt quite comfortable with this assignment. As he walked, he whistled a tune. He surely didn't want anyone to be startled by his approach, especially if they were desperados and had any reason to be leery of strangers.

As he got near the tents, he shouted, "Hello, the camp!"

In less than a minute, the flap of the tent was thrown back, and Newly found himself looking down the barrel of a rifle.

Newly stepped back and said, "Hold on, hold on there."

"What do yah want?"

"Nothin,' jest tryin' to be friendly. I figured you fellers was caught by the water and probably was short on supplies. I had a little extra coffee and know how it sure warms a man's soul and makes his misery easier to tolerate, so I brought yah some, if you'd like."

"Yah got any whiskey?"

"No, but I wish I had. It sometimes works better than the coffee to ease the pain." Newly followed his statement with a good-natured laugh.

"You're sure right about that," the stranger said. "But the coffee will do in a pinch, so come on in and let's chew the fat."

Newly held out the small sack of beans as he entered.

There were four men in the tent, all setting or sprawled out in as comfortable of positions as they could get.

Newly started off by introducing himself and offering a friendly handshake. Each man introduced himself and returned the hand. They visited for a few minutes about the rains and the weather and how it had slowed their journey.

Newly finally said, "I got to get back to the wife and kids. I sure hope you can find some kindlin' and get some of 'em beans a workin' over a fire. I'll wish yah a safe journey."

Newly entered the tent where Bass was waiting for his report.

"Well, looks like our luck has changed. All of 'em fellers is on the list. Nothin' big, jest whiskey runnin', and one of 'em is wanted for horse thievin'."

"Well, the rain may have served us well after all. Looks like the water is droppin', and probably we can cross tomorrow. So tonight, I'll jest slip over there and see if we can't put 'em in our load."

They both chuckled and waited to see what nightfall might bring.

***

The next morning, their load looked more respectable than it had, and they were able to ford the waters and head to Fort Smith.

When they entered the town, there was a feeling of unrest and despair amongst the people on the street. Bass attributed it to the weather and continued to the jail. He knew that too much of anything was unsettling. When he had left, there was the same feeling, but it was because of the never-ending heat.

He did his usual procedure of making sure the men were secure and headed toward the office to start his report. As he entered the area, he was met by Marshal Crump who motioned for him to come into his office.

Bass entered, and Crump uneasily nodded for him to take a seat.

"Bass, I got some bad news for you. I had instructed that none of the others tell you this, because I wanted it to come from me. I know that you and Larry Keating were good friends, and I just wanted to be the one to tell you that while you were gone, Larry got killed."

Bass sat for a moment making sure he had understood the news. He then looked at the marshal and asked, "How'd this happen?" He knew his job and did it well. I can't imagine him gettin' sloppy and lettin' someone get the drop on him."

"It was Cherokee Bill that got him. That bastard should have already been swingin' in the breeze, but the Supreme Court had ordered a new hearin' for him, as they have for all of those murders that are crowdin' the jail."

"Good Lord! We go out and work our tails off bringin' 'em in, and those fellers up there that know nothin' of this land want to stall the cleanup. How did it happen? Weren't they secure in the basement?"

"Well, more than Bill had to have been involved, cause someone tripped the brake at the top of the cell doors on Bill's side, and all he had to do was push it open. The setup started first with the trippin' of the brake, but was aided by the fact that paper had been stuck in Dennis Davis"s key hole, which made Turnkey Eoff get his key hung while he was tryin' to get him secure. He told Larry, right then and there, that somethin' was about to happen.

"When Larry stepped forward to see if he could help, Cherokee poked a pistol through the bars and told "im to give 'im his pistol. Larry knew that if he surrendered his weapon, that things would really be out of hand. So, he went for his sidearm. That murderin' son-of-a-bitch Cherokee, killed him, right there on the spot. He not only shot him once, but twice before Larry turned and still staggered clear down the corridor. I don't know if he was tryin' to help Eoff or get away or keep Cherokee from gettin' his gun. Whatever it was, it was a testament to his bravery and courage. The last thing he said was, "I'm killed."

"Then George Pearce ran out of his cell with a chair leg and was gonna knock the hell out of Eoff for the key. This might have been Eoff's lucky break 'cause Cherokee couldn't get a shot at him for fear he would hit Pearce. Before Pearce reached Eoff, George Lawson fired at Pearce from the stairs and drove 'em back.

"Cherokee and Guard McConnell exchanged point blank shots, but neither got hit, and Cherokee ran back into his cell, where he must have had a stash of bullets 'cause he kept on firin'. It weren't long until the whole floor was full of smoke. All the guards could do was fire at the puffs of smoke that Cherokee was a sendin' their way.

"The prisoner Henry Starr, I think you know him, he is some relation to Belle, finally volunteered to go get Cherokee's gun if they would jest stop shootin'. I think he and all the rest in there started thinkin' that one of 'em was gonna get killed if the shootin' continued. The guards promised, and I guess Cherokee had had enough, so Starr came out with his pistol.

"You know there was over one hundred rounds fired before this thing was over, and it is a wonder that more guards or some prisoners weren't killed."

Bass sat and tried to visualize the events and then said, "The day they stopped Bill's hangin' was a sad day for this country and a really sad day for Larry's wife and family.

"You know, Larry was some kind of special person. He always treated me nice, and he had even had me to his house a couple of times to meet his family and have a meal with 'em. I'm havein' some problems dealin' with this mess.

"What did the Judge have to say about this? I'll bet he is a raisin' holy hell." Bass said.

"Bass, he was on a trip to Saint Louis when this happened, and you are exactly right, he is as mad as I have ever heard of him bein'. He got interviewed by the St. Louis paper about this, and he had a passel to say.

"If you'd like, I'll read you what he said. I got a copy of the paper here, and since you have been involved in bringin' in so many of those waitin' for their hangin', I think you ought to know what is takin' place. It's kinda long, but I am so pleased he said what he said."

"I'd like to hear what the Judge has to say. I wish he was here, 'cause I'd like to hear it from his mouth, but if you would read it, I'd appreciate it."

Marshal Crump reached into the middle drawer, of his desk and pulled out a newspaper that showed the wear of many readings. He laid it on his desk where he could get the full source of the sun.

"Parker says, 'What is the cause of such deeds, do you ask? Why, the cause lies in the fact that our jail is filled with murderers, and there is not a sufficient guard to take care of them. There are now fifty or sixty murderers in the Fort Smith jail. They have been tried by an impartial jury. They have been convicted and have been sentenced to death. But they are resting in the jail, awaiting a hearing before the Supreme Court of the United States. While crime, in a general way, has decreased very much in the last twenty years, I have no hesitation in saying that murders are largely on the increase. This has been noticeable, chiefly in the last two years. I attribute the increase to the reversals of the Supreme Court. These reversals have contributed to the number of murders in the Indian Territory. First of all, the convicted murderer has a long breathing spell before his case comes before the Supreme Court. Then, when it does come before the body, the conviction may be quashed, and whenever it is quashed, it is always upon the flimsiest technicalities. The Supreme Court never touched the merits of the case. As far as I can see, the court must be opposed to capital punishment and tries to reason the effect of the law away. That is the sum total of it. First, the guard at the Fort Smith jail ought to be doubled. In speaking as I do of the Supreme Court, I am mindful, of course, of the wise and merciful provision of the law which declares it is better than ninety-nine guilty ones should escape than that one innocent man should suffer. Nor am I devoid of human sympathy, because I have endeavored to carry out the law justly and fearlessly. But sympathy should not be reserved wholly for the criminal. I believe in standing on the side of the innocent. Take that man Keating. He was a quiet, peaceable, law-abiding citizen. Is there no sympathy for him and for the wife and children who have been deprived of his protection and support? Wasn't his life worth more to the community and to society at large than the lives of one hundred murderers? If one man can shoot another in self-defense, cannot the third, representing society, extend its protection in a similar manner, though, of course, in a strictly legal and judicious manner? Now as to the condition of the Indian Territory in the matter of murders: these are confined, to a great extent at least, to what I call the criminal intruders men who have committed crimes in the States and come to the Indian Territory for the purpose of refuge. Take the resident population, and it is as orderly and as quiet as any to be found anywhere. During the twenty years I have been involved in administrating the law there, the contest has been one between civilization and savagery, the savagery being represented by the intruding criminal class of which I have spoken. I have never found a time when the Indians the Cherokees, the Osages, all of them have not been ready to stand by the courts in the carrying out the law. The United States government in its treaties, from the days of Andrew Jackson down to the present time, stipulated that this criminal element should be kept out of the country, but the treaties have only been made to be broken. The same treaty was made when the last strip was purchased. But this is the old story over again. Thus, the criminal class keeps on increasing; its members marry, and the criminal population keeps on ever growing larger. A criminal example is set to the young Indian and so crime spreads. But were it not for this intruding criminal class, the Indian Territory would be fit for statehood today. During the twenty years I have been sitting on the bench. I have only known of three cases of mob violence. Prisoners have been brought to the court from a distance of three hundred to seven hundred miles. The reason is that the people have confidence in the court and the laws, and in this, there is a great object lesson. I used an editorial from the "Globe-Democrat" the other day in charging the grand jury. The editorial commented on the laxity of the courts in carrying out the laws, and it hit the nail on the head. At the present time, there seem to be a criminal wave sweeping over the country, the like of which I have not seen before. It is due to the laxity of the courts. I have this much satisfaction, after my twenty years of labor; the court at Fort Smith, Arkansas, stands as a monument to the strong arm of the laws of the United States and has resulted in bringing to Indian Territory civilization and protection.'" the marshal concluded his reading.

Bass said, "Well, he sure didn't back off from things I've heard him say in the past. You know my son works for him, and we've had several conversations when I was visitin' his house. He is one tough and dedicated man, and I am proud to call him my friend. Jest sayin' the word friend makes me think how many I've lost over the years.

"I guess they have already laid poor Larry to rest. I sure hate it that I missed the service, but when I get cleaned up and finish my reports, I'm goin' over and tell his wife how sorry I am. I had a fifty-pound bag of flour and a fifty-pound bag of beans left in the wagon from this trip, 'cause I didn't get much of a load this time. I think I'll take that over. I know they are gonna have some rough times soon."

Crump said, "That's a good idea, and I think I'll ask some of the other deputies if they would do the same. I'm sorry I had to tell you this, and I am sure that she will appreciate the food."

Chapter 8

The Murder Trial

Bass went about his work as usual. Day in and day out he traveled the Territory in search of law-breakers, but he had a really bad feeling about the new head U.S. Marshal Carroll. The man had been a Confederate officer, and, to make things worse, he was a Democrat. This appeared to be a perfect combination for trouble. To date, nothing had happened out of the ordinary, but Bass felt that each time he came in contact with Carroll, that a chill filled the room. In spite of this, he felt the only thing he could do was to continue his work with his same dedication and try his best to steer clear of the man.

Bass had just finished his run after being on the road for over a month. He had returned to Van Buren in hopes that his presence might help bring his children some feeling of family. He knew, too, that his wife needed some help with the discipline of the boys. The farm was in good shape, and the horses looked as good as he could remember. He had spent the last two days settling into a more normal life, when he saw Marshal S.J.B. Fair ride into his yard and dismount.

Bass was in the barn, observing the new colt that he had for so long awaited. The horse had the look that Bass had hoped for, so he was proud that Fair had arrived in time to inspect the new arrival. Fair had always been friendly, but he had never visited the farm, and Bass thought it good that the marshal's visit had come at such a time of festivity.

Bass turned from the horse's stall and started toward the house. a broad smile on his face as he observed Fair's arrival.

Marshal Fair dismounted and looked directly at the house, seemingly hesitant before making his next move. The man removed his hat and slapped it against his leg,rewarded with a cloud of trail dust. He then carefully returned it to his head, never taking his eyes from the front of the dwelling. As he slowly walked to the rump of his horse, he stretched and flexed his legs to get the feel of the earth back under his boots. In what seemed like a reluctant move, he reached into his saddlebag and removed some paper. Bass then saw the marshal pull his pistol out and check it before returning it to his holster.

Bass was taken aback by this last move. This was the thing that a marshal does when he is expecting trouble, not making a friendly call.

Fair now began watching Bass as the two men began walking toward each other.

"Fair, I'm glad you're here," Bass said when he got closer to the marshal. "You got here in time to see the new arrival I had been telling some of the boys about, and now you'll be able to tell 'em about it."

"Bass I'm afraid you won't be glad to see me after what I have to tell you." He looked at the ground for a moment and cleared his throat. After hesitating, his eyes fixed on Bass. "I've got an arrest warrant here for you."

Bass looked puzzled. "What did you say?"

"I'm sorry, but I have an arrest warrant for you for first-degree murder, and I am told to bring you in dead or alive', and I sure don't want any trouble."

"The murder of who?"

"One William Leach."

"That happened over two years ago, and everyone knows it was a accident. Why in the hell are they just bringin' this up?"

"Bass, I've no idea, and I'm only doin' what I was sent to do. Now, all I ask is that you come along with me peacefully."

"I'll do that," Bass said."I can't wait to get back to Fort Smith and find out what this is all 'bout. Let me go to the house and get some clothes and tell the family what is happin'."

"OK,you can do that, but don't be long. And please don't bring your guns out. "I want this to be peaceful."

"Don't worry. I know you're doin' your job, just like I've done mine for years. I know this is some kind of mistake, and I sure don't want to do anythin' except gettin' it cleared up."

***

When they arrived at the federal jail, Marshal Fair escorted Bass to the reception desk and said, "I've brought the prisoner Bass Reeves in and am now turnin' him over to you. I want to say for the record that he was no trouble."

Jim Carlson, the head jailer, kept his head down, not wanting to make eye contact.He fumbled with the papers on his desk and acted like he had never admitted a prisoner in his life. He finally filled out the form, after having to scrap the first one because of mistakes.

Finally, he looked up and said, "Bass, I'm just doin' my job. I don't like this one bit. You've stood there more times than anyone I know, except it is totally different this time."

Bass said, "Jim relax, I won't be here more than a day. I know you're doin' what you have to do. I've asked Fair to go get me a lawyer, and as soon as he gets here, everythin' will be straightened out."

"Bass, you know that this has put me in a real bind. According to the rules, I'm supposed to put you in the maximum lockup downstairs. But you have put about ten or twenty per cent of 'em murderers down there, and I know someone will get killed if I do.

"So, I'm goin' a put you in a holdin' cell and hope your lawyer gets here quick, and we get this mess straightened out fast. Now, if you would follow me."

***

Bass was pleased when Bill Clayton appeared at his cell. Bass had worked with the attorney many times, and, in fact, Clayton had come to Bass' home in Van Buren several times to discuss cases.

After the greeting, Clayton said, "Bass, I wish this thing was as simple as it should be, but they have several sworn testimonies that you blatantly and viciously murdered Leach in cold blood."

"That's crazy. He and I were friends, and I have carried the burden of his death every since it happened." Bass paused, " Who's made these charges?"

"Mary Grayson, James Grayson, and all the others you had in the prison wagon."

"Well, that's even crazier. First off, none of 'em saw what happened. They were all in the tent secured for the night, secondly. I had all but Mary in custody, and most of them I'd brung in before. How could anybody take the word of these scoundrels? They don't have a honest bone amongst 'em."

"The problem is that the commissioner has believed them for some reason. If we don't take this seriously, you could spend the rest of your life in prison or, worse yet, get hung. I will tell you, I'm really suspicious of these charges. In the past, any of the marshals that had a like problem were charged with manslaughter, or the worst I can recall was second-degree murder. They have charged you with first-degree murder.

"I feel someone is after you, and it has to be coming from some place high. Now, let's get down to business. I want to bring McCravens and Marcum in on this. I want all the brain power I can get surrounding me." Clayton paused and then said, "Bass, if I do this, it is going to cost a lot of money."

"I got a little in the bank," Bass said. "But I sure don't have enough for all of you guys. I guess I could sell my horses and farm, but I sure would hate to do that. I've worked all my life for that, and I sure would hate to give it up and deprive my family the comfort and security they need."

"I know, but what would their comfort and security be with you gone?" I don't want to make any decisions for you, but this could get real challenging, and it is your life that is at stake, and if there are people in high places after you, the trial may not be fair."

"Bill, I've been around the courts too long and seen what happens to folks that don't have good lawyers or who don't pay attention to what they're told. Let me think 'bout it and get back to you."

"I at least have one piece of good news for you," the lawyer said. "I've gone to Judge Parker, he is very upset with these charges, and has given an order that you be placed on trustee status. That means that you will probably do some cleaning up around the jail during the day and be housed at night here on the first floor. I also have asked for a bond hearing, so I can get you out of here. The problem with that is that they hardly ever set bond for a first-degree murder charge. Now you see why it is going to be expensive.

Chapter 9

On the Street

It was a long and expensive struggle to get Bass freed on bond. His freedom came after six months, and then with orders that he could not leave the city limits of Fort Smith or he would be put back in jail and lose his trustee status.

Bass had known many a prisoner facing similar charges who simply rode away. But he was glad to at least be free from the confines of the jail. He reasoned that Judge Parker had not only taken an unusual length of time to hand down the order, but had made it restrictive to keep from looking like any favors were being played.

His freedom came at considerable expense. Bond had cost him three thousand dollars, plus he had attorney fees, not helped by the continual request for delays because of the difficulty in locating important witnesses, Bass quickly drained all of his funds. Then he was forced to sell his farm and most of his horses. He was now free, but broke.

He wondered if the freedom from jail was worth the loss of all his years of work. The legal moves and requests had come one at a time, making his arrival in a financial mess sneak up on him. But once it had set in he became more hostile.

He knew these charges were made up by those who resented him for the work he had done, but the fact that they had gone on for so long made him know that someone in a high position was behind the charges.

Marshal Mershon came to his rescue, providing Bass a place to stay. The marshal also was continually keeping his ear to the ground and trying to pick up any news that could help in Bass' defense.

Mershon had been Bass' friend since first going to work for the service. Helping Bass in this time of need had proven what a real friend he was.

While grateful for his freedom from jail, Bass suffered from the loss of his freedom to travel. He had often thought about the life of the average man and how boring the daily grind of working at one location must be, not to mention the unchallenging jobs he thought most people had. Now he was trapped into an even worse situation with the order that he not leave the bounds of the city, and he had nothing to keep him occupied.

He was fortunate, however, to have friends and supporters who often came by or who would visit with him on the street as he tried to occupy his time.

On one of his outings, he dropped into the City Hotel saloon with nothing particular on his mind except to get away from the boredom of his isolation in the room furnished by Mershon. He saw some friends, John Williams and Dave Pompey. They visited for some time, discussing nothing of great importance, talking about things like the heat and discomfort that the June weather had brought. Then A.J. Boyd walked to the table. Evidently drunk, he pulled out the only empty chair at the table and plunked down.

A.J. grasped Bass by the shoulder and leaned toward him, A.J.'s breath delivering the final evidence that he had consumed far more liquor than he should have. With a firm hand on Bass' shoulder, A.J. first squeezed his shoulder and then shook Bass with some force. He then said, "Now, Bass, tell me your side of this here murder. I don't want no brief tale. I want to hear it all."

Bass reached up and dislodged the grip that the drunken man had so disrespectfully placed on his shoulder.

"I've no intention of discussin' this matter with you. You set on the jury, and you know that it is forbidden for me to discuss my problems with you. I'll tell my story to you and all the others at the proper time and place, but 'till then, I'd kindly ask that you not speak to me in any way what so ever. You first of all have no right to ask me questions, and, secondly, it is plain to see that you have had way too much to drink."

A.J.'s manner now became hostile. "Listen to me, you black son-of-a-bitch. You will talk to me, or I'll see to it that they stretch your neck till your tongue hangs out. I've got at least three of us on the jury that are sick and tired of a nigger runnin' around actin' like he is somethin' special."

Bass was shocked at the man's hostility, but took his time before responding. "Well, you may threaten me all you want, but I ain't tellin' you nothin'. I want a fair trial, and I think I'm hearin' that that ain't possible. Now I would suggest, for your own good, that you leave."

A.J. stood and with his cane, he tapped Bass on the shoulder, with some force and said. "I have done told you what is gonna happen to you if you don't answer my questions. I'll be damned if I'm gonna let some murderin' nigger escape what he deserves."

Bass decided to try a different approach. "If you want to discuss something, tell me something. Deer, cows and horses all eat grass, but a deer shits small pellets, and a cow shits big flat cakes, and a horse shits big round balls. Why is that?"

A.J. looked at Bass for some time, slightly swaying, trying to grasp the change in conversation. Finally, he said, "I have no idea."

Bass replied in a voice that everyone could hear, "Then why should I discuss anythin' with a man who doesn't know shit?"

A.J.'s mouth fell open, and he swayed again, then turned and staggered to the door.

John said, "Bass, you sure shut him up, but you got a real problem there. I want to congratulate you for not takin' his head off, but you got to go to your lawyer right now and get that stupid drunk off of the jury."

Dave sat shaking his head. He took a drink from his beer and said, "I agree. This man can be the death of you. John and I will stand by you on what just took places. So, go see Clayton and get that son-of-a-bitch taken care of."

Bass shook his head and said, "You fellers are right. I can't take the chance on him poisonin' the jury. I feel lucky that you fellers were with me and was a witness to this, and I thank you for your support."

Bass pushed himself away from the table, took his leave and entered the heat of the day. He glanced up and down the street and observed those bold enough to be challenging the heat. He wondered what their day was like, hoping theirs were going better than his.

Bass straightened his hat as he walked towards Clayton's office. Thinking about his encounter with A.J., he finally concluded their meeting was a blessing. If this hadn't occurred, the trial may have gotten underway with his fate in the hands of people who were ready to find him guilty without even hearing the facts.

After Clayton heard the story, the lawyer immediately went to Parker and had charges brought against A.J. Boyd.

The judge took quick action after hearing both David and John confirm Bass' story. Each had a little difference in their testimonies, but combined, they painted a scathing picture of Boyd's character and ability to serve on a jury.

Boyd's' only defense was that he did not remember the conversation, and that if it did take place, it was due to his drunken condition.

Judge Parker was not impressed and stated, "You have stained the moral force of a strong federal court, and I hereby find you guilty of contempt of court and dismiss you from any and all jury duties. I also fine you fifty dollars and put you on a year's probation. I highly recommend that you change your ways and ask God to help you get back into the fellowship of man. Your conduct is a disgrace to Justice, and I don't take kindly to any man who lets their personal lack of self control shade fairness."

***

October came, and Bass was more than anxious to get his legal business out of the way. All of the legal stays had drawn the matter out far too long. He had not questioned the stays, because he knew that he had the best legal team that money could buy. At least he knew he had paid them enough that they should be the best.

Bass felt very strange seated in the accused chair. He had been in the courtroom so many times as a witness that it was like home, but to be sitting in the accused chair gave him a whole new feeling for the courtroom.

The room contained supporters and haters, but most were reporters or people who just wanted to say they had watched this important trial take place.

When Judge Parker entered the courtroom, all came to their feet and stood until he took his familiar place behind the tall desk that gave him total visual command of the room.

Prosecuting Attorney Forester called Mary Grayson as the first witness.

Forester asked her to describe what took place the evening of the shooting. She proceeded to tell that Bass had shot Leach after an argument about Leach letting a dog, that had wandered into camp eat from his cooking pans. She said that Bass told Leach to get rid of the dog or he would kill him and Leach had told Bass that if killed the dog, Leach would kill Bass or his horse.

The woman said she then watched Bass pick up his Winchester, put cartridges into it and shoot Leach without any warning.

"What happened to Leach then?" Forester asked.

"Nothing he just fell down," she said.

Bass listened as the prosecutor presented witness after witness, until finally he couldn't listen any longer. He disconnected from the proceeding.

Meanwhile, each of the prosecutor's witnessed painted a picture of Bass as an angry, hostile man who coldly shot an unarmed man because of an argument over a dog.

Clayton, however, brought a totally different story to life. He established that Bass had allowed Mary Grayson in the camp because her husband was ill and she wanted to care for him. She confirmed that Bass had even furnished her husband a horse to allow him to seek medical attention.. The defense attorney established that Bass and Leach were friends who had worked together several times, and that they were known to talk harshly to each other in playful relations. She and the other witnesses confirmed that after the shooting, Bass had comforted the cook and done all he could to save the man who survived for more than a day with a wound in the neck. Witnesses agreed that if Bass had wanted to kill Leach, he was too good of a shot not to have fatally hit his target and from a greater distance than the accidentally shooting Bass claimed. The defense attorney even established that Leach had suffered for many days with diarrhea and was in such a weakened condition that the gunshot wound may not have caused his death. The attorney further destroyed the reputation of the witnesses by showing that none were able to see the events, and that all were either related to a prisoner or a prisoner, most with criminal records. He concluded that the witnesses were simply trying to cast dispersion on the man who was bringing them to face penalty.

When Bass took the stand, he told of his friendship with Leach. He told how he regretted the accident, describing how it happened while he was trying to remove a .45 cartridge from his .44 caliber Winchester. He could not explain how the discharge happened, but described how he had worked on dislodging the improper cartridge for several minutes before the accident.

It took the Jury only a few minutes to return a verdict of not guilty.

Chapter 10

Ringing a Belle

The crew was surprised when they noticed that Bass had taken Blaze out of retirement and rode him to Fort Smith. He had left instructions for them to be ready to the depart station on exactly October the 10th and had been most insistent on that date. In fact he had been so insistent that all of his party thought that he must have had a date with a lady. They had never seen him so worked up over an exact time, as they knew that they would be on the road for at least a month and thieves hardly ever did things in the spur of the moment.

Kenneth, his cook for the outing, had know Bass for years and had cooked for him on at least three forays into the Territory, finally said, "Bass are you turnin' into some old woman or somethin'? We ain't never seen you so worked up over nothin'." Of course he smiled when he said this, he sure didn't want to get the man anymore uneasy than he was.

Bass looked at him for a moment and then a smile came to his face. He then replied, "I am sorry I just have a deadline to meet and if I miss it things want be good."

Kenneth laughed and said, "You got a date with a lady or somethin'?"

Bass turned his head toward him and flatly said, "It's somethin' like that."

This answer really caused Kenneth to stop in his pursuit of answers. He had never known or heard of Bass womanizing and the fact that Bass would even respond in this way had shocked him.

The subject was dropped and the crew made sure that they left town in the early morning of the tenth. Bass was riding Blaze and this also became part of the mystery. None of the crew had seen him ride this stallion for over three years. He had told them that Blaze had been retired and was only used as a stud. He had also brought Lightnin' and had secured him to the back of the prison wagon.

It wasn't that unusual for him to drag an extra horse, but usually it was a very indistinctive horse that he would ride when he wanted to disguise himself as some down trodden traveler or cowhand in order to pull off a surprise infiltration into a suspect's camp or homestead. Lightnin' sure did not fit that mode or operation.

Finally his posse man Milo Creekmore said, "What is goin' on? Bass, you're actin' kinda strange this time out, and me and the boys are a little concerned."

"Ain't nothin' to be concerned about. I just gotta a date with a lady, and I don't want anythin' keepin' it from happenin'."

Creekmore now was as stunned as Kenneth. He had ridden with Bass twice before and he had often visited with other posse men about their experiences with the deputies they rode with and womanizing had never come up when Bass was talked about. Many of the other deputies had drinking, gambling, women and even thievery in their stories, but Bass had always received the highest of marks among the stories on morality.

After a long day on the trail Bass said, "Let's camp here for the night. I know it's not the usual place, but I really could sure stand a change of scenery."

Creekmore and Roland Nave, the other posse man, set to work preparing camp as quickly as possible. Kenneth scurried into the surrounding trees to gather wood for the evening meal. All of these men seemed to work at a little faster pace than usual, due to the strange happenings of the day. They had barely finished the set up and Kenneth had not even got a pot of coffee on the boil when Bass said, "Gentlemen, I have to leave you now. I should be back by midday tomorrow. You should break camp early in the mornin' and head toward Okmulgee. I'll pick up your trail and catch you when I can. If I don't get there before it is time to make camp tomorrow night go ahead and set up. Roland you and Milo know the area and we got some warrants for some fellers that live right close there. Just go on and pick 'em up, but go together. I know no one on the list should be hard arrest, but you never know and I sure don't want anyone hurt."

After this speech, which was, by far the longest of the day, Bass went to the back of the wagon and led Lightnin' over and mounted Blaze. He tipped his broad brimmed hat and hurried off into the dusk.

As he rode into the final moments of the sunset the crew all stood and watched in amazement. They had never heard of Bass doing anything like this and they were now more puzzled than ever as to what was taking place.

Milo finally said, "Well, boys, he is the boss, and it's best we do what he says. I sure think he is old enough to know what he is a doin', and it ain't none of us's business. Let's get some eats on and make it a night."

Bass was enjoying his ride on Blaze. It had been far too long since he had set atop him and it brought back many memories of the past chases and close calls the two had shared. He kept Blaze at a steady pace and approached Younger's Bend.

Bass had over the years had several visits with Belle. Most of them had been in Fort Smith when she was there shopping or arranging bail for one of her friends. However, there had been a few occasions where he had stopped in at Younger's Bend. These were usually cordial and Belle had really learned to like and respect Bass and the feeling was mutual. They had often talked of family and friends and while most of the time the friends were on different sides of the fence it made little difference to the two. Their conversations always included their love for horses and Bass never tired of Belle talking about music and things of culture. They were so foreign to him and this was the only place beside Judge Parker's house that he was exposed to it and he knew he wanted more.

Another thing on Bass' mind was the trouble that her son Eddie Reed had gotten himself into. Bass could not fault her too much, because he had problems with his own boys. He felt that this gave him some better understanding of what she was going through, and he planned to talk with her about it.

Belle had always shown Bass great respect. This respect had come from the fact that Bass had always done what he said he would do and never gone to Younger's Bend to arrest people. He only stopped as a friend. This of course does not mean that from time to time, if Belle desired to talk about persons who she did not like, that Bass did not listen.

As he got near he could see there was a warm glow of lamp lights shining through the windows and a few horses at the hitch. He had thought he had heard music as he had approached but the wind had only allowed it to filter through the air from time to time. The closer he got the clearer it had become. It was the sound of a piano and Belle's voice that now was coming in louder and clearer.

A smile started to creep across his face the closer he got. He had not heard a piano in some time and sure had not heard the fine female voice that was singing in tune with the sweet notes.

Bass was glad Belle was happy; it signified that the evening was going to be most pleasant. He only hoped that the horses tied in front did not represent the presents of people who did not want to see him and vise versa. But he felt sure that Belle know he was coming would have cleared the establishment of undesirables. This date had been planned far too long. She had never had problems removing those she did not want and tonight would certainly be one night that she could be choosy.

Bass approached the house and both Blaze and Lightnin' shook their heads, twitched their ears and snorted as they smelled the air. He slowly dismounted and eyed the horses tied beside him. He did not recognize them and that made him feel a little better he surely did not want anything that would spoil this night.

Bass cautiously entered and when he opened the door the sweetness of Belle's voice became even more pleasant. Her ability on the piano was startling. Here they were in what should be considered the wilderness and she was filling it with beautiful harmony.

As Bass stepped into the room Belle looked up from her activity and even missed a note or two, but she recovered and politely nodded and tilted her head in the direction of an empty table with three chairs.

Belle was dressed in her finest. She had on a long flowing purple gown that had a plunging neckline and her head was covered by a stunning white hat that had a matching purple plume reaching toward the ceiling. Her well coiffed hair protruded from under the brim of the hat and Bass knew that she had gone through a tremendous effort to look special for the evening. The one thing that marked her as Belle Starr was the two pearl handled pistols that were more than evident hanging on her sides with the handles reversed they made it look like they had been color coordinated with the deep purple of the gown.

While she was playing the door opened again and a tall man entered. He sported an outstanding Stetson hat and a flowing duster jacket. His boots were polished to a bright shine and it was obvious that he had an outstanding waste coat and matching paints under the jacked. He certainly didn't look like a cow hand in fact he didn't even look like a banker. He looked more like a very successful card shark that had just stepped off of a riverboat after cleaning everyone at the table.

Belle looked at him and smiled and nodded for him to take a set at the table that Bass was setting.

In just a few more notes Belle ended her performance and stood up from the piano. She turned toward the men in the room and was greeted by applause and bravo's from all there.

She smiled and walked to the table with the two strangers and held out her hand, which was immediately grasp and kisses placed on it by both men. She reached down and picked up the bottle setting on their table and very gently refilled both glasses, smiling all the while.

When she finished she curtsied and thanked them then turned toward the table were Bass and the elegant man were setting.

As she approached the stranger stood and grasps her hand and placed a gentle kiss on it. He then reached up and placed a warm kiss on her cheek. Bass also stood, but when she offered her hand he simply took it in his hand and it completely dwarfed hers.

Belle said, in a very lady like way, "May I join you gentleman?"

The stranger pulled out the empty chair and helped her locate herself comfortably at the table. When finished both Bass and he took a seat.

Belle said, "I am so glad you are both here. I have wanted you to meet for some time."

She turned to the stranger and said, "This is Bass Reeves, the marshal I have written you about on several occasions. Bass this is Jim Keller my cousin from Carthage, Missouri. Well, he is not from Carthage anymore. He hangs out down in New Orleans most of the time."

The men exchanged handshakes, and in doing so, appeared to be sizing each other.

Jim said, "Well, strange situations surely make strange bed fellows. I would have never thought

it from cousin Belle, but if she says you're alright that is sufficient for me."

Bass said, "I'm sorry. I'm just a little caught off guard here, but it is a pleasure to meet one of Belle's family."

They visited for a while and it turned out that Jim was exactly what he looked like. He had spent the last several years riding the steamers up and down the Mississippi playing poker and when he wasn't on the river he had a small gambling house in the quarters in New Orleans.

Jim said, "Not to change the subject, but I am a great horse fancier and I just saw two of the biggest and impressive studs standing at the hitch when I arrived. I really like to bet on the horses, and they both look like they could really do well on the track. Who do they belong to?

Bass said, "They're mine. When you are as big as me a small horse is as useless as a preacher in a whiskey joint fight. I pride myself in havin' outstandin' horses for my work."

Jim laughed. "Well, that explains it. If you ever want to get rid of them let me know. I own a few great runners on my little place in New Orleans."

Belle finally said, "Jim would you mind joining my other guest and keep them entertained. You might even get a game started at the table. Bass and I have something we have talked about doing for a long time and I think tonight is the night."

Jim replied by exiting the table and extending his hand to the two men setting at the other table, and was quickly in deep conversation.

Belle said, "Bass are you ready? And do you think tonight is OK. I think that all is ready."

Bass said, "Well, we never know until we try, and I like doin' it at night. If you think things are ready we can try."

Belle said, "Set here for a moment and let me go and change my clothes into something more appropriate. I'll be right back."

Belle returned in a much shorter time than Bass had expected. She had changed into riding pants and a blouse with a light, matching jacket. She also had a lit lantern in her hand.

"Let's do it," she said.

They exited the house and walked to the hitch. Bass removed the saddle and blanket from Blaze and draped it over the hitching post.

Both Blaze and Lightnin' were tossing their heads, switching their tails and constantly stomping their feet.

Bass took Blaze by the reins and followed Belle as she walked toward the corral.

When they got to the gate, she held the lantern high.

"Well, there she is. Isn't Dorothy beautiful? She's got some age on her, but she is as sound as she ever was."

They were immediately greeted by the magnificent face of a sorrel mare. Her nostrils were flaring while she was tossing her head and slowly snickering. She was quickly joined by more stomping of hooves and the twisting and turning of Blaze as he started to release low grunting sounds and his nostrils flared as he smelled the air.

"Bass said, "Looks like you had it timed just right. You truly are a woman that knows her horses."

He opened the gate and removed the bridle from Blaze. There was no need to ask him to enter. In fact, Bass and Belle had to move with quickness to keep from getting trampled in Blazes dash.

The night air was filled with the sounds of snickers and whines. The stomping of feet and the rapid movement of the two mating animals seemed to echo through the trees.

From time to time Belle would raise the lantern high and observe the action. She finally lowered it and said, "Let's let them play for a while. I always liked that."

After about thirty minutes, Bass said, "I'll get him and take him to the barn. I'll give him all the oats and water he wants, and tomorrow, about noon, we'll repeat this."

Belle said, "Give him plenty. We sure don't want him shootin' blanks. I think this is the last colt I will let her have, and I hope you are right, that it should be superior."

"He ain't known to shoot blanks, and it is a real pleasure to think that I had the chance to see the filly I sold so long ago and to complete the plans I had for her years back. I always thought that this would be the perfect matin'. The mixture of King, my old English mare and Blaze should be exceptional, but only time will tell."

Chapter 11

Eddie Reed

The next morning Bass arose from his sleep in the barn early. He fed Blaze again and walked him into the early morning sunlight. Bass made sure that he was sound, but it was evident that the smell in the air was enough stimulant for Blaze, and he had no need for pampering. He tossed his head in the air and his nostrils flared as he continued his search for his new conquest.

Bass said, "Easy, feller. We're gonna wait till about noon before we let you have another run at 'er. I know you think you're ready now, but let's let you get totally refreshed 'fore you take another run. I promise you, she'll be awaitin'."

Bass took him back into the barn and placed him in the stall. He then went to where Lightnin' had been housed and spoke to him, after making sure he had plenty of grain and water.

"I hate it boy that I had to drag you along on this trip. I know it had to be very disappointin' to you, but I worried that the lady might not be ready, and I would need to leave Blaze here. If I'd had to do that, I would a needed you to get back on the road. Maybe next time it'll be your chance."

After the chores were done, Bass went to the house to have some breakfast. He had partaken of the food provided by the house before and had always been more than pleased. However, he really wasn't that concerned with the quality, because anytime he could get a home-cooked meal when he was on the chase was a plus.

He was greeted by Belle. She was dressed in casual attire, very similar to the previous night, but it was evident that she had primped and done everything she could to look her best.

That was the way of this woman. She sure had her wild and aggressive side, but always cared for herself like a proper lady.

She said, "Bass I have had you a special breakfast prepared. You sure have earned it. I am so excited about getting my mare breed to Blaze that I just don't think I can stand the wait to see the outcome.

"It was my pleasure. You know once I had sold her I regretted it. I knew she had the blood and I wanted this matin' to happen. So I'll be nearly as anxious as you to see the results.

"Is Jim goin' to join us for breakfast?"

"I doubt it. As a matter of fact, I doubt if he gets up before you leave. His life is so orientated to the nightlife that early mornings escape him. On top of that he rode a long way yesterday and I know he is dog tired."

After several minutes of pleasant exchanges, Belle said, "Bass I got a problem that you might be able to help me with. My boy Eddie has got himself into two scrapes with the law and it really concerns me. I know I'm not the best example for a kid, but I also know as his mother that I don't want him to go through all the crazy times and tribulations I have gone through. Now he and I don't see eye to eye on a lot of things. In fact, we have nearly come to blows from time to time, but I still care for him.

"On top of that it has started hurting others I care about, and that really concerns me. It seems that his sister has gone to selling herself over in Van Buren and Fort Smith to raise enough money for his lawyer fees and fines.

"I respect her for wanting to help, but that is not a proper way for a lady to conduct herself and I am somewhat ashamed of it. Again, I've got to say that I haven't set the best example for her, but I was raised proper and schooled proper, and I had hoped that at least my kids would turn out better than me.

"Maybe, I was hoping for more than I should have. I know that my influence sure didn't help these kids, and the men I have let hang around them has made the problem worse.

"Is there something that you could do to see if you could get Eddie straight? He has always thought a lot of you, and you are the only person I know and trust on the right side of the law."

Bass sat for a moment and finally took the napkin from the table and wiped his face. He then took a drink of coffee and cleared his throat. "I'm honored that you would come to me with this serious a problem, but I probably ain't got the right to advise anyone about their kids. I have a passel of 'em, but my wife and mama has done most of the raisin' and, like you, I've spent far too much time doin' things that I liked rather than bein' the father I should a been.

"You talk about bein' ashamed, and I must be right there with you. I got two boys that has been sent to prison, with me supposed to be the man of law and order. I take that to be a real failin' on my part, and I ain't got no excuse for that.

"But Belle, I'll tell you what I'll do for you. I'll talk to Judge Parker about Eddie and see if he can come up with somethin'. My boy Newland works for him, and he has had a run-in with the law in the past.

"I know you don't have one good thing to say about the man, and he feels the same way about you. But he is a just man, and a man who really cares for people. He works his self to death and still has time to do a lot of things for Fort Smith. He just hands down the law as it's written 'cause that's his job."

"Bass, I'm just looking for some relief, and I can't be choosey where it comes from. If you can get something done to change this situation, I'll be forever beholding to you."

Bass looked at his watch and said, "I've enjoyed the meal and am happy that we had one good thing come out of our meetin'. I promise you that I'll talk to the Judge for Eddie and see what can be done, but I need to get to the barn and let Blaze have one more go at the mare. Then I need to be on the road."

Belle rose and stuck out her hand and as Bass was shaking it, she said, "I am glad you have done what you have done, and I know you will do what you can for Eddie, and you're right, you need to be going. I have some guys coming in here today from Missouri that I don't want you and them to get together. I'm afraid if that happened, I would lose too many friends."

Chapter 12

So Long Ben Billy

Bass returned to the site were the night's camp had been established. He knew that he was later than he had intended to be, but felt that the kindness he had done for Belle would be repaid some day in some way. He had always tried to keep people who knew people as friends, and it had paid off many times.

He picked up the trail and put Lightnin' at a fast pace. He had decided to ride him this day due to the fact that Blaze had put in a good night and day's work. The trail was clear, and he had an idea where the camp would be.

He broke over a ridge and entered the small valley were the creek meandered and provided a good amount of shade from the willows and elms that stood on the waterways shore. Just as he had assumed, the prison wagon was there, and the cook fire was ablaze. The aroma of the evening meal filled the air. It was then that Bass realized that he had not eaten since the great breakfast provided by Belle.

Kenneth stepped back from the pot he was working over as Bass approached, and the cook lifted the spoon in the air as a sign of greeting. His eyebrows rose, and his face showed that he had already painted a mental picture of what had caused Bass to be late.

Bass rode Lightnin' to the rear of the prison wagon and was pleasantly surprised to see that two people had already set up occupancy in the facility.

When he dismounted and was working with Lightnin's rigging, he spoke to his unhappy guests. The response he got was not pleasant, but he had not expected to be welcomed with open arms. So he just smiled and said, "Gentlemen, the good news is that while you're in my care, you'll be fed and housed for free. The bad news is that we're a long way from home, and your stay in that wagon will probably put blisters on your asses."

After he got the horses tended, he walked to the fire. Kenneth put out his hand, after wiping the splatters of soup off, and said, "Glad you're back. We have had a right good start on this trip. Nave brought these two in 'bout ten o'clock this morning. They were packin' four bottles of whiskey each. Said it was as easy as pie gettin' the goods on 'em. He went out after a little bit to eat and was supposed to meet up with Creekmore at a crossin' down the road. They supposedly has got a lead on a guy named Bob Billy."

"Know the name, and he has a price on 'im," Bass said. "It'd be a real start if we could get that man in the bank. You got anythin' to eat? I have been on the road since a early breakfast and ain't had a bit."

Kenneth said, "Got a couple of biscuits left from breakfast, if that'll do you for a spell. I'll have some soup in about thirty minutes."

"Sounds fine."

Bass took two biscuits and squatted down next to a tree. He was just starting to get comfortable when Creekmore and Nave rode up.

"Hey boss, how'd it go?"

"Went just like I had hoped, and I see you boy's are off on the hunt at a good pace."

Creekmore said, "Yah, but that is just the start. We think we know were Bob Billy is, and it's less than a day's ride."

The next morning, they broke camp and traveled toward the supposed hideout of Bob Billy. On the way, they heard a shot off to the west and turned in that direction. Shots often meant that their services were needed.

When they topped the ridge, they observed four men skinning and quartering a cow They approached slowly, and the men seemed so enthralled in what they were doing that they had not even noticed the strangers approaching until the posse was nearly at their side.

Bass asked, "What you fellers up to?"

The men looked up from their work, and one said, "Nothin'." He was holding a huge slice of the critter in one hand and a knife in the other.

"That your cow?"

"Sure is."

"Why didn't you butcher it close to the house?"

"Just didn't have time."

"I doubt that. I'm takin' you and the critter into custody until we can get this straightened out."

Creekmore and Bass loaded the fresh meat and hide, with the brand, on their horses and escorted the surprised thieves to the wagon."

They continued on to their destination and had Kenneth pull the prison wagon into a clump of trees about a mile from the reported hideout.

Bass said, "Set up camp here. The luck we are a havin' on this trip makes me think that it's gonna be a great month. We may just have to work out of this area for a few days, so set up good."

Bass, Creekmore and Nave made sure the prisoners were secure and that Kenneth was in total control of the situation. They mounted and headed for the hideout.

The hideout was a small hovel, surrounded by a split rail fence. There was a soothing grove of trees for wind and sun shelter and the homestead had a field in the rear. The place looked like most of the humble dwellings that occupied the area.

It belonged to Tom Barnett and Bass had known him for several years. They had crossed paths, but Bass had never arrested him. However, Bass had always suspected that the man had more than a sodbuster's income.

Bass dismounted and walked toward the house with his Winchester in his hand. Creekmore and Nave stayed mounted.

Bass reached the rail fence and shouted, "This is U.S. Marshal Bass Reeves, and I have a warrant for Bob Billy, or Bob Williams as he is sometimes known, and I understand he is in the house. I'm askin' that he come out and come with me peacefully!"

Bass was always at the ready, but was taken by surprise when Tom Barnett stepped out on the porch and immediately fired his Winchester at him. This was followed by Bob Billy rushing out the door and sending a volley in Bass' direction.

Bass hit the ground and took cover behind the fence. Creekmore dismounted and ran toward a small stand of trees just outside the fence. He fired at the resisters to draw them away from Bass, as they had continued to rain a hail of bullets toward him.

Bass held his fire. He had not come to take a life. All he wanted was to take Bob in, and he could not understand why Barnett had joined into the fray.

Bob turned his Winchester toward Creekmore and fired at least three times. His shots were taking great chunks of bark from the tree that Milo was using for cover. The closeness of the shots showed that Milo was now in great danger.

Bass had tolerated this as long as he could. With the safety of his posse man in mind, Bass raised his Winchester and fired.

The shot hit home, squarely in the center of Bob's body, causing him to slam against the wall of the hovel.

Barnett turned and ran into the house immediately. In seconds, Bass saw him exit the back door and jump the fence, running at full speed across the field.

Bass shouted. "Milo, get mounted and cut him off 'fore he gets into the woods!"

Bass then walked slowly toward the house, still at the ready. He knew that his shot was good, but sometimes snakes can strike in their dying breath.

He looked at the body and knew there was nothing to fear, so he entered the house. He found several bottles of whiskey and Barnett's empty Winchester lying on the floor.

He returned to the porch and waited.

Milo soon appeared with Barnett secured with a lariat around his waist, begrudgingly walking behind Milo's horse.

Milo sat in his saddle and looked at the lifeless Bob Billy. "Well, he asked for it. You know these fools should learn one day that it'll probably be the last thing they do when they fire on you. But I guess there ain't no one around after that happens to tell the story. He was a makin' it pretty hot for me, and I thank you for the relief."

They went to the back of the house to continue their investigation and found a horse tied there that was far too fine to be owned by either of the culprits. This and the whiskey must have been the reason for the unexpected resistance from Barnett.

Bass shook his head and said, "What a waste. Billy would of only got a few years in the jail. Now he has got a eternity in hell."

Chapter 13

Paris

"Bass, the federal district court has become so large and the caseload has become so heavy that new courts have been set up in different locations. It is my pleasure to assign you to the new court in Paris, Texas," said Judge Parker.

"Judge, you know that I've a little problem with that. I don't know that I ever told you, but I've been ordered by the court there to never come back into that place," Bass said.

"Why was that?"

"I shot a man there when I was a slave, and they was gonna hang me. I did it to protect a lady. She was the daughter of my master. My luck was that he was also very important and he backed me, and the man I shot was a low life varmint that had no backin'. My master got the judge to let me go if I would never return to town. This was before the war, but I was soon involved, gettin' in and goin' to the fight.

Parker smiled. "Bass, that was a long time ago, and I have the right and responsibility to place people where ever I choose. I think that the place needs you, and on top of that, you will be working out of there, but most of your work will be back across the Red River in your familiar grounds. It will just mean that whoever you snake out of there will be jailed and stand trial in Paris.

"On top of that, it might be good for those folks to have to cater to a black marshal. I know you, and I know you will do credit to the office and won't be anything more than an asset to the courts there."

"Well, sir, I have served you as best I could and as often as I could, so if you think I will make a fit there, I guess it's my duty to do as you ask."

"Bass, I wouldn't send you if I didn't think that it was a good choice. You know how much I respect you and your commitment to the law."

"Well, sir, if that is what needs to be done, then I will be on my way tomorrow."

The two men shook hands, and Bass replaced his broad-brimmed hat. He stepped to the door and said, "I am gonna hate not seein' you as often as in the past. You have been a real friend, and I won't forget you."

"Bass, you know the feeling is mutual. I have never had a marshal that I had more faith in and been prouder of. Now, keep up the good work and have pride in your country, for your country sure has pride in what you have done."

Bass left the next day and traveled through the country that had become so familiar to him. He had a slight sadness as he traveled. This had been his territory, and he knew it like a book.

As he continued his journey, he also thought of how far he was going to be from the Mankillers and his home in Van Buren, but he consoled himself by knowing that his job was to serve, and if the Judge wanted him there, he needed to be there.

As he entered Paris, a smile crossed his face. He started to recall how many trips he had made into town with Master Reeves and how many times he had been in so many of the familiar stores. He had sold the master's vegetables to most of the stores and had accompanied Nancy into most of the others, to help with her packages.

He also recalled that this was the place where he first had thoughts of his enslavement' and how he had started to think about why he was not free and what made him different than the people he had seen walking, talking and dealing on the streets.

His reminiscing stopped as he noticed the number of people who were curiously staring at this strange black man who exhibited great confidence in his approach. They seemed both confused and concerned at his appearance.

They had seen many a black man walking a mule or skinnin' a team, but had never witnessed a black man astride a fine horse and carrying two pistols. It was a sight that left most frightened and uneasy.

These feelings disappeared when they observed him dismounting in front of the federal jail and enter as if he owned the place.

Marshal Shelby was sitting at a desk doing paper work when he entered. The marshal laid his pen down and rocked back in his chair. He looked for a moment, and then rose and extended his hand.

"Well, marshal, I am certainly glad that you have got here. I have been waitin' for you and have a passel of work lined up for you. Don't worry with unloadin'. I'm sendin' you back into the Territory. You know Calvin, up in the Choctaw Nation?"

"Yes, sir, I been there many times. I know the land and people real good."

"I figured you did. That is why I'm sendin' you there. We have horse thievin', muderin' and robbin' goin' on there like you won't believe. I was just waitin' for the right man to come along to get that area under control, and it sure looks like the Judge has sent 'iim to me.

"You know, if you don't want to ride up, I can get you passage on the railroad and save you some wear and tear on your horse and body."

"Marshal, that sounds like a nice change. Lightnin' and I probably would like that."

"Then consider it done. The train will not leave until in the mornin', so you might as well make yourself comfortable."

"I just need to get somethin' to eat and get Lightnin' in the livery. I'll stay the night there and be ready for a relaxin' trip in the mornin'. Do you have any instructions for me now?"

"I know about you, and I know what you can do. All I want you to do is telegraph me with reports from time to time and get that country cleaned up any way you can. If I need more from you, I will telegraph you."

"OK. I would like to take a little stroll around the town before I eat. You know I used to come here often. I was a slave then. Times have sure changed."

"I knew you were. I guess you know the town then, so I will let you go and do what you want. I'll have your ticket brought to the livery."

Bass and Shelby shook hands as they parted ways.

Bass stepped from the jail and into the daylight. He looked slowly up and down the street. He walked to Lightnin' and led him down the street. The place seemed to have changed greatly, not in buildings, but in names and the decor of the buildings.

He placed his horse in the livery and made arrangements to spend the night there. Then he strolled down the street slowly. He made sure that his badge was clearly visible on his coat, before he started the journey.

The thing that struck him first was the size of the city. He could recall how he thought that it was the biggest place in the world, and how he believed that nothing could compare to it when he first started coming there as a boy.

He also recalled how he remembered the length of the streets and how grand they were then. Now they were just ordinary in size and length, and he was taken aback by his remembrances of the past. He finally got to the site where his most unforgettable event had taken place.

He shut his eyes and clearly remembered crossing the street behind Miss Nancy, carrying her packages. He could still see himself following her as she stepped up on the boardwalk as he noticed the drunken Watson approaching.

His mind was filled with those few seconds that had made such a change in his life. The swaying movements of Watson and his blatant disregard for Miss Nancy, and, ultimately, the brief struggle with Watson, that had resulted in Bass shooting him in the shoulder.

He had thought of this moment in his past life several times, but it was so vivid now that it felt like yesterday.

These thoughts made him stop and wonder what had happened to Mr. Maxey and Sheriff Olson. Then he realized that these events had taken place more than thirty-five years ago. None of these people could still be around, and if they were, he would not know if they even remembered him.

He sure remembered them. Mr. Maxey had provided the legal services to get him freed from jail, and Sherriff Olson had protected him from the lynch mob. This also made him recall Master Reeves with more admiration than he could remember summoning for some time.

He finally turned from the sight and entered a store. He walked to the back of the store and asked if they had some ham. As the butcher was carving off a pound, he nearly cut his finger because he could not keep an eye on Bass and at the same time do his work.

Bass asked the butcher, "How long have you lived here?"

"All my life. Why?"

"Well, sir, I was just wonderin' if you remember a man named Reeves? He lives east of here on a farm."

The butcher cautiously replied, "Why do you want to know?"

"I know him in the war."

The butcher then noticed the badge displayed on Bass's coat and relaxed.

"Well, he ain't with us no more. He was an important man to this state and to this here town. Even was Speaker of the House of Representatives in Austin, but his dog bit 'im and gave 'im the mad dog disease, and he up and died a terrible death."

Bass stood in silence. He looked at the floor and stroked his mustache as he took in the news.

"Is his daughter still on the farm?"

"You sure know a lot about these folks."

"Well, I was their slave in the past and even served with 'im in the war."

"You were their slave and now you is a marshal? That's amazin'. But as far as his daughter goes, she ain't here no more either. She up and got hitched to some feller, and they moved away. I don't know where, just moved away."

Bass returned to the livery, checked on Lightnin', then brushed the horse down. Afterward, he went to the loft to eat and think of the news he had received.

Chapter 14

Calvin

Bass left the next day, and the trip by train was a great relief. He had traveled by train on several occasions when he was assigned to deliver prisoners to the Detroit Federal Penitentiary. These trips had always been boring to him, but the fact that he had been able to see territory that seemed so foreign and unreal had changed his vision as to what a civilized country could be like.

Of course, the size of Detroit had also changed his prospective of city life and what it had to offer. He had relished his stays in the big city, but never felt comfortable there. He knew that his place was in the open country where he could enjoy nature and the freedom to ride where and when he desired.

Now he was faced with new challenges. Here, he was alone, and his duties were to enforce the law. He served warrants and took prisoners back to Paris to face their charges. These were things that he had always done, but it just did not feel the same without Fort Smith and Judge Parker.

He developed a friendship with Dr. Jesse Mooney, who he first met at Younger's Bend. Dr. Jesse, as he was known, lived close by. He knew nearly everybody and became a great source of information. The duties of a country doctor had caused him to travel all over the area. He was called on frequently to assist the good and the bad. The doctor was something like a marshal, in that when people needed him, they really appreciated his work.

The one place where there seemed to be an abundance of murder and skullduggery was a placed called Corner. The only establishment there was a saloon, but what a saloon it was. The violence was so great there that they had their own cemetery behind the building for those unlucky enough to enter.

It was told that many a traveler had made their last stop there, if there was any chance that they might be carrying a small poke. Murder seemed to be one of the major industries for the city and its saloon.

No law had ever ventured into the area and none of the saloons regulars figured they ever would. Those thoughts were soon overturned when Bass was assigned to Calvin. It was his job to enforce the law and this seemed the place where it needed enforcing the most.

His first trip to Corner was to find a man named Asa Goings. He had been told by Doc Jesse that Asa was often there, and that he was one of the most dangerous of the group of villains that hung out there.

Bass saddled up his new horse. He had brought this new stallion from the farm and felt that he was ready for action. He had seen him work and knew his heritage and that was impressive. The fact that he was white bothered him, but his speed and endurance had impressed him enough that he had named him Lightnin'.

This Saturday morning he didn't only have Asa's warrant but his saddlebag was full. If this place was as bad as he had been told, he might do a month's work on just this one trip.

He approached the town with heightened senses. His experience told him that if he was going to accomplish his goal and make an impression on the villains of the area, he had to strike hard and fast. He knew that they would not be expecting him and hoped that the element of surprise would give him the edge that he needed.

Bass dismounted in front of the saloon and instinctively checked to make sure that his pistols were free and smooth in their holsters. He walked to the entrance and pushed open the swinging doors.

As he entered, he was greeted by several people's eyes, whose faces displayed disbelief that a Negro would have enough courage to enter their domain. They were even more shocked when he calmly announced, "I am U.S. Deputy Marshal Bass Reeves, and I've come for a man named Asa Goings."

The room was filled with silence, for several minutes. Then the small group of men started to smile and then laugh.

"You say you is a marshal, and you wants to take Asa in?" a patron snarled and another started to laugh. "You must be out of your nigger mind, if you think you can do that."

"Well, friend, I don't think I'm crazy. As a matter of fact, I'm positive I can do what I said, so if you will point him out to me, I'll be glad to show you."

At this moment, a slight man of about twenty-five stood and

said, "They don't have to point me out. I'm right here and hankerin' to see you take me in."

"You are sure you're Asa? I don't want to be botherin' the wrong man."

"I'm Asa, and it's no bother."

"From what I hear of you, wouldn't you feel more comfortable if I turned my back to you?"

"You son-of-a-bitch!" Asa shouted as he reached for his pistol. His speed was exceptional. He cleared leather faster than Bass and let loose a shot that struck Bass in the leg. Unfortunately for Asa, Bass did not miss his target. His .45 slug struck Asa in the forehead. The projectile snapped the man's head backward, and in an instant, the soles of his boots were displayed to the other occupants of the room as he fell to the floor, with his legs tangled in the chair where he had been sitting.

Bass slumped to his right as he felt the pain in his left leg, but he kept his eyes on the room and his pistol leveled at the shocked occupants.

"Now, it would be my advice that they rest of you stay calm, unless you have a desire to join your friend. I have come here for one man, and that is all I aim to take, this time. Next time I come, I expect a little more respect and hospitality.

"Now, two of you fellers need to get hold of your friend and carry 'im out and put 'im over his horse, as I am gonna take 'im in just like I said I would."

As two men struggled with Asa's body, Bass pulled his bandana and wrapped it tightly around his leg, never taking his eyes from those that were assisting him in fulfilling his duty.

When they finished, he said, "Now, you boys get on your horses and get goin'. I don't want to see anything but a cloud of dust behind you."

Bass turned to the bar-keep and said, "I'll take over your bar. There won't be any customers for a while, and you go get Doc Jesse. If you don't want to do that, I'll burn this hell hole to the ground, understand?"

The bar-keep pulled his apron off and threw it on the bar. "You promise you won't burn it down, and I'll go."

"I promise, but you had better be fast 'bout it or I may change my mind."

The man hit the door running, and in about thirty minutes, Doc Jesse entered with his black bag in his hand.

"Bass, I figured someday you'd be needin' my service. What happened here?"

"Just a feller that didn't want to do what I asked."

"How many times have you been shot over the years?"

"First time. I've had a lot of close ones, but this is the first time I been hit."

"From what I hear, he must have been pretty fast to beat you."

"Was, but that's only half of the challenge. More important is to hit what you're aimin' at. I guess it is too late for 'im to figure that out now."

The doc laughed as he prepared to probe his tweezers into Bass's leg. "You sure you don't want a slug of whiskey? I think it would be on the house."

"No, just get it over with."

After examining the wound, the doctor said, "Bass, you were a lucky man, in one way, and not so lucky in the other. The slug didn't hit that main artery or you would have bled to death, but it is so close that I am afraid that if I try to remove it, I might be the one to cause it to rupture, and that would be the end of you. What I am going to do is leave it right where it is and give you some medicine to take and tell you to stay off of it for at least a week. Then you can start using it limitedly. Now, Bass, if you don't let that heal, you stand a good chance of dying. I will come by your house everyday to check on you and make sure it doesn't become infected. You are a lucky man that the first man to shoot you didn't end up being the last man to shoot you."

"I just figured that things happen like they is supposed to, and if it had meant to have got me, it would've."

After Doc finished putting everything back in his bag, Bass said, "Thanks, Doc what do I owe you?"

Doc shook his head and pushed his hat back. "I usually get three dollars for this kind of operation, but I support your work, so it's on me. The only thing I ask is that you don't shut this place down. I make a good part of my livin' because of what happens here."

Bass laughed and said, "It probably would take me bein' here full time to shut this place down, so don't worry."

Bass turned to the barkeep and said, "I don't wanna have to come back, but if I do, you had better get this place in order. You understand me?"

"Yes, sir."

Outside, Bass made sure the body was tightly secured on the horse. Honoring his injury, he had to mount Lightnin' from the right side. It was an uncustomary move for him and his horse, but he got it accomplished.

As he left Corner, he hated that he could not stay around and try to seek out others that he knew had to be in the area. However, the ball in his leg was starting to cause him great discomfort, and he knew it would possibly slow him down and give his prey too big of an advantage. Time would take care of his leg, and those he was after seemed to be never ending.

Chapter 15

A Message from Home

While Bass was nursing his wound, he sent for his sons to come and help him. He really didn't need help he just wanted to spend a little time with his children. He was greatly looking forward to the reunion and hoped that it could serve as some kind of healing between his boys and himself. He realized he had spent too much time away from them and his mother and wife. But times were hard and he felt he had to keep up the pace in order to make their lives easier.

As soon as Bass heard the train whistle, he headed to the train station and anxiously awaited its arrival. He was glad now that he had been wounded and could hopefully use this time to heal not only his leg, but some of the stress that he knew his sons were having.

After limping to a spot on the platform, he stood, looking into the windows as the train slowed and finally came to a stop.

What a great moment this was going to be. He had spent so little time at the home place. In fact, all he could remember was going there, visiting with the help, checking the horses and sharing a meal, before he had to leave.

The train finally came to a stop and let out its last gasping hiss of steam. The conductor stepped out of the passenger care and placed the step on the ground. An elderly gentleman grasped the handrail, and the conductor steadied him as he placed his foot on the portable step.

Bass limped down the platform so that he would be squarely in front of the door. From here, he would be able to see all of his boys as they departed the train. He waited, but no one appeared. He stepped closer and strained his eyes into the darkened doorway. Nothing appeared to be moving. Bass then walked up to the door and stared inside. Again there was no sign of movement. He turned to the conductor and asked, "Was there a bunch of Negro boys on the train?"

Two fisted justice

The conductor looked at him and said, "I never saw a bunch of boys on the train, and I have come all the way from Fort Smith. Besides, if they were Negroes, they wouldn't be on this car."

"What do you mean?"

The conductor stared at him and focused on his badge. "There ain't no Negroes allowed on this car. When a train starts in Arkansas and they have no cars for Negroes, then no Negroes are allowed on the train. I'm sorry, Marshal, but today this was the only passenger car."

Bass dropped his head. His disappointment was greater than he had imagined. Then he consoled himself with the thought that they probably had missed the train and would be in tomorrow, when a second car was added.

He turned and started to limp back toward his rented room. His slow motion was interrupted by a shout.

"Papa, I'm here."

Bass turned and saw Newland jump from the door of a cattle car. When he had gained his footing he slapped his hat against his leg and then shaped it a little and returned it to his head. He walked down the platform and looked at the boards as he approached.

Bass turned and saw his lone son, Newland.

"Where is all the others?" he immediately asked."

Newland lowered his head down and said, "They ain't comin'. I was the only one that wanted to."

"What do you mean that you were the only one that wanted to?"

"Jest that, Papa. All the others said they didn't have time to come, but one of us had to, so they picked me. Well, they really didn't pick me. I volunteered. I was needin' to get out of the area for a few days."

Bass's face turned stern. He now glared at Newland. "What the hell is going on here?"

Newland looked at the ground and pushed the toe of his boot into the dirt. He kept his eyes down and softly spoke, "We jest thought that you don't seem to be able to come home much, and if you can't work in time for us, we don't need to make time for you."

Bass reached out and grabbed Newland by the collar. He jerked his head up and looked directly into his eyes. "I'm your father, and I deserve more respect than that. I work hard to see that you'll have what you need, and I expect you to be thankful and appreciate that."

Newland could barely speak. The grip on his collar also had placed shuge knuckles against his throat. "Well, Papa, we jest doesn't think you think of us much. You only come home when you want to, you only stay as long as you want." Newland rasped.

"I can sure see why they sent you. I guess you're the only one that has the grit to talk to me like that."

Bass then released his grip and looked at the ground. He stood in silence for a while and then said."I guess you're right. I sure don't spend much time at home." He paused for a minute and then said, "I don't know how this came about. I don't know what to do about it. I don't have an answer for you, your mother or the others. All I know is that I is in over my head in this here work, and it jest is in my blood.

"Not that I don't think about you kids. It is just that I just can't seem to let things go here. I got people that depend on me, and I can't let 'em down."

"But, Papa, we depend on you, and you never are there. We is so used to you not bein' there that we jest don't seem to miss you."

"What a terrible thing that to say. I love you kids, and I work for you kids, and I need to help clean up this country for you kids."

"Papa, we don't give a damn about this country, and all we know is that it takes you away from us. So in truth, we hate this country."

Bass turned his back on Newland and took a step away from him. He pushed his big black hat back on his head and stared into the nothingness of the countryside. He stood for several minutes and then turned.

"Well, I'm glad you're here, and I'm glad you spoke. I think I need to ponder what you said for a while. Now why was you in the cattle car? You should have plenty of money at the house."

"Oh, we ain't got no money problems, but I can't buy a ticket on the train. They don't let no Negroes ride on this train if it only got one passenger car."

"I ride the train anytime I want to. What the hell are you talkin' 'bout?"

"Papa, you is different from us and all the other Negro folks. You wear a badge and got more rights than any of the rest of us Negro people. In fact, I'd guess that if you didn't have that star on, you couldn't get on the train either. So it's not you that is ridin' the train — it's the star."

"I put my life on the line nearly every day, and I have served this country well, and you mean to tell me that my kids can't ride the train?"

"That's right, Papa. We can't ride the train. We can't go to the big school at home, and we can't vote and you can't either. You maybe helpin' this country, but who for? Do you realize that those fellers you put in prison, when they gets out, they can ride the train, but your family can't? Do you realize that most towns you ride into hate you and would show you how much they do if you weren't wearin' that badge?"

"Awright, awright, you made your point. All I can say to you is that

Two fisted justice

your grandma taught me a long time ago that you gotta do right. She said that because all the others is doin' wrong, that don't make it right. And that if you is the only one doin' right, it don't make it wrong. That is all I can say on the matter. I know I'm doin' right, and I will keep doin' right as long as I'm able.

"Now about me doin' right at home. I see where I been wrong there. I shoulda been home more. I sure shoulda been closer to you boys. But you gotta know that I ain't had no papa, and I don't know how to be a papa. All I know is work and the law. I try to do the things I know, and if that ain't good enough, I'll have to try harder at the things I don't know.

"Son, I don't fear death, but it sure looks like I should fear losin' my family. I will have to work on that if you all 'll give me a chance."

"Papa, we want you home. We need you home. Do you realize how scared we are that you'll come home some day in a box?"

"Newland, you has sure brought me a message. I guess I should say I'm sorry and hope all of you can forgive me for my short comin'."

"Papa, please don't hate me for tellin' you this. We jest want to be a family."

"Now, Newland you said the reason you came is that you needed to be away from the area. What's the problem?"

"It's jest a little thing, and it'll pass. There is some people that think I stole some stuff, and it ain't true. I figured if I got away for a while, it would all settle down."

"You say it ain't true. Is that the truth?"

"Yes, Papa, that's the truth."

"Then that's the end of that. Let's go to the house and get me off of this leg for a spell."

The next morning Bass said, "You know, son, there is some right nice catfish in that lake on the edge of town. I'd be right proud if you and I went down there and tried to reduce their numbers."

Newland replied, "I'd be more than happy to. You know, if we do this that, it will be the first time that you and I have done somethin' with just the two of us."

"Well, son, let's just say that I want you to come with me, and, hopefully, this will be the start of somethin' good for all of us."

Chapter 16

Unpleasant Reunion

Bass rode slowly. He was in no hurry to fulfill this obligation. There had been too many good things that had come of this relationship, and he was very uncomfortable with what he was going to have to do. But, he knew it was his job, and he understood why he had been chosen.

As he approached Younger's Bend, he was comforted by the fact that there were no horses at the hitch. He wanted as little attention to this matter as possible. He cast his eyes toward the corral and saw Belle standing there with a bucket in her hand. She was alone and obviously simply was watching the horses consume their daily rations. This is one thing that people who love their horses do. Some people call it watching them grow.

The sound of his approach caused Belle to turn and look his direction. She already had reached for her pearl handled pistol, but when she recognized him, she immediately released the handle and moved her right hand from the aggressive position to her hat, tipping it back on her head.

She started walking toward Bass with a reassuring smile on her face. She was swinging the empty bucket like a school-girl, merrily going to school. She even had a slight skip in her gate.

Bass approached slowly, and when he got about twenty feet from her, he pulled his horse to a stop and dismounted. He immediately tipped his hat and closed the distance. He extended his hand to grasp the one being offered.

"Bass, I am so happy to see you. What a pleasant surprise. "

"I'm happy to see you, too, Belle. How've things been goin'?"

"Pretty good. Come on over and let's sit and talk. It has been far too long."

She lead the way to a bench under the shade of a large pine tree and said, "Sit your old bones here. I am sure that it is more comfortable than sitting in that saddle. I'll go to the house and get us some tea. You just sit and relax."

Before he could respond, she had rushed to the house and quickly returned.

Still smiling, she said, "I put some mint in it. How does it smell? I hope you like it."

Bass lifted the hot cup to his nose and said, "Nice, very nice." Then he took a sip and cradled the cup in his hands.

Belle seemed to be full of energy this bright and warm morning. She would not let Bass get a word spoken before she started another friendly statement.

"Bass, I just want to thank you again for all the things you have done for Eddie. I was really impressed that you not only talked to the Judge, the old son-of-a-bitch, but that you got him to appoint Eddie as a marshal. He tells me that he has worked with you several times and that he really likes the work and is especially pleased with all the help you have been to him. Tell me about something you have done together."

"I would a figured he had already told you some stories."

"He has, but I haven't seen him for more than six or seven months, and I'm sure there has been something that you have worked on since.

"You know he and I have this love hate relationship. I love him for being my son, but he and I clash about as much as two people could, from time to time.

"So I have to get my mother's pride from hearing about his success from others. Go on now and tell me a story."

Bass was relieved that Belle wanted to spend some time exchanging pleasantries. It would give him time and a better opportunity to explain his unexpected visit.

"Well, Belle, we just a while back worked a case that was really a great example of what he can do, and I hope he continues to develop his skills as not only a marshal, but as a detective.

"We got sent a few months ago up to a place close to Keokuk Falls. There had been a murder, one Zachariah Tharch from Arkansas. You might a known him. He was a well respected man and traveled all over these parts."

"Zach? "Yes,I knew him. He was a really nice man, and he had stopped in here a time or two. Always conducted himself like a gentleman. I'm sorry he got killed. We can't be losing those kinds of people, but go on with the telling."

"Seems as though he had hooked up with a feller from Tennessee, who was of bad character his a named Wilson. I don't know why that happened, but it did.

"Wilson was seen in the Red Dog saloon, drinkin' heavy, and later that night he was seen with Tharch at a camp outside of town. Sometime in the night, people heard two shots. A few days later, some people found Tharch floating face down in Rock Creek. The body had got stuck in a bunch of driftwood or he would a ended up goin' down the North Canadian River, and probably never seen again.

"Two of his fingers had been cut off, and his head had been split open with a ax. It was a real upsetting sight. The catfish had got 'im and really made a mess of 'im.

"After Eddie interviewed several people, we decided that Wilson had to sure be the likely suspect, so we set out to trail him down. We found him up on the Kickapoo Reservation a couple of days later. We hauled him back and he identified Tharch, or what was left of 'im, and Wilson claimed that Tharch was his uncle and that Thrach had sent him ahead, with the wagon and team, while tTarch stayed back and did some huntin'.

"Eddie jumped right on this and kept askin' Wilson about his kin and all of that. The more he asked him, the more confused Wilson became. He finally said the two really wasn't related, but that they were just the best of friends.

"Eddie kept right on 'im and finally Wilson said his name wasn't really Wilson, but was Casharego, and he had done time in Tennessee.

"I was real proud of the way Eddie had twisted this guy's story until he just seemed to give up.

"Eddie searched high and low and finally found a blood-stained ax hidden under a bunch of supplies in the wagon. He asked Wilson how it got there, and he said he had no idea. Eddie also saw some traces of blood spatter on Wilson's boot, and he tried to say it was from a rabbit he had killed that morning and ate for breakfast.

"Eddie and I went back to the old campsite, and Eddie noticed that there'd been two fires, and said that was really unusual, especially since one of 'em was against a tree. So he went to probin' around in the ashes next to the tree.

"If you remember, a while back we was so dry that jack rabbits was havin' to pack a lunch to cross the county. Well, this dry weather had caused the ground to split right were the fire was, and after Eddie scooped out the ashes, there was a big crack in the ground.

"There was what looked like blood in that crack, so we dug it up real careful and saved the evidence in a saddlebag.

"We took Wilson to Fort Smith, and with the evidence that Eddie had found and us testifyin' about the situation, Wilson was found guilty. The Judge did what the law calls for and sentenced him to hang.

"The Judge ordered that the sentence be carried out, and in no time,

Wilson was hung. Eddie and I were at the hangin'. It seemed like a fitin' end to our work."

When Bass finished, Belle just sat there. He could see in her face a look of satisfaction in that her son had taken on a job and done it well.

She said, "Well, my boy did well, and that is all I want to know. He puzzles me most of the time, but at least you have got him to doing something, and for that I am grateful."

They continued to visit, the conversation being mostly about the horses. The center of the conversation was the fact that Belle's mare Dorothy had delivered a strong filly and that Belle now had her in training to race.

As time passed Bass felt that he could no longer postpone the unpleasant task that was at hand. He cleared his throat and said, "Speakin' of horses. You know that there has been a lot of talk about horse thievin' goin' on, and some of the talk has your name tied to it.

"I know that I've promised you that I would never come here and bother your friends without you sayin' it was OK, but I got a warrant for your arrest, and the Judge sent me 'cause he felt that you'd be more willin' to come back peacefully if I was the one to serve it. I feel very uneasy with this, but I've a job to do, and as you know I take my job seriously. So, I'm askin' you kindly and as a friend to come along with me to Fort Smith. You know that they have hauled you in many a time, and you've always come out alright, and I hope the same is true this time, but I think you should know that from what I hear, they have a pretty strong case, so you better get your best lawyer on it."

Belle tossed her head back and leaned back on the bench. She looked directly into Bass' face and her eyes narrowed. She started to speak, but seemed to pause in order to get her thoughts collected. After a silence that was only broken by the sound of the birds in the trees and the gust of winds that were making the pines sway, she said, "Bass, I have not stolen any horses. I am guilty of nothing except having friends that the law has it in for, but I will tell you what I'll do. I'll come into town with you and let them present whatever case they have and be back in my home before you can skin a cat."

"Belle, you know I don't want nothin' less. I just have a job to do, and it is up to other powers to see what takes place after that. I hope you don't take offense, to what I've done and we can keep on bein' friendly."

"Bass, you are a man that I respect, and you have done right by me. I hold no hard feeling toward you and kind of feel honored that at least they have sent the best to get me.

"Now, if you will give me a few minutes, I'll go to the house and get my stuff packed. I don't plan on being in town long, but you know us ladies want to look our best, and without a few carpetbags of stuff, that would be impossible."

Before she turned to the house, she stopped and turned to Bass. "You're not going to put cuffs on me are you?" She then broke out in laughter, as she saw the confused look that covered Bass' face.

Chapter 17

The Color Divide

Bass had just finished breakfast when a strong rap on his door brought him to immediate alertness.

He went to the window and looked out, keeping back from the window and in the shade of the early morning darkness that filled the room. He had become more and more cautious with things like this. There always had been those who wanted to take him down, but he had received word that at least two men in the last week had been bragging in Keokuk Falls that they were going to be the ones to put an end to the "nigger marshal "and that it was coming soon.

From what he could gather from the report, they were two of the men he had sent to the Judge, and they had ended up in the institution in Detroit.

His source had not gotten their names, but had said they looked tough and well capable of carrying out their threat.

Bass had taken the warning seriously, but also had laughed at the description. He had sent far too many to the Judge, and many of them had sworn on the trip to Fort Smith that if they got sent up, they were going to come back and kill him.

After being satisfied that the man at his door was the runner from the telegraph office, Bass opened the door, but kept his .45 in his hand.

The runner let out a little gasp as his eyes went from Bass' face to the Colt that was now dangling at his side, and said, "Marshal, I'm sorry. I should a told you through the door that it was me and I had a message from Paris."

Bass looked at the Colt, and then laid it on the table by the door, and said, "I'm sorry if I startled you. It's just that a man can't be too careful now days. Would you please read it to me?"

"Yes, sir, Marshal." He cleared his throat, held the yellow piece of

Judge Parker & Bass Reeves

paper in front of him and read, "Come immediately to Paris. Stop. Prepare to stay. Stop. Take precautions on trip. Stop. Riot in process. Stop. Marshal Dickinson."

Bass said, "Thank you." Then he handed the man a quarter, "I hope I don't scare you." He then closed the door slowly.

Bass packed his saddlebag. It did not take him long because he always was ready to move in a moment's notice. He picked up his carpetbag and looked inside. This was his long trip backup, always at the ready. Still, he opened it and did a final check to make sure he had all he needed.

He also needed to go to the store to get supplies for the road. He looked out the window to see if the store was open yet. As he looked, he noticed two men ride up to the hitch in front of the store and dismount.

Bass leaned closer to the window and strained his eyes. He was not sure, but he thought that he remembered one of the faces.

His interest was heightened when he noticed both men moved cautiously and were continually looking directly toward his house. They both pulled their guns from their boots, and Bass noticed that the one in the gray vest had a shotgun.

Each man stepped to the boardwalk and were exchanging words and pointing in different directions. Finally, the one with the rifle started across the street and went out of Bass' view. The other slipped into the walkway between the store and the funeral home, all the while keeping his eyes turned toward Bass' house.

Bass grabbed his Winchester and went out the back door. He turned to his left and hurried down the side of his house and through the yard of his neighbor's house. He circled that house and crouched by the porch next to the street, where he was out of sight.

He waited and watched. Time seemed to move slowly.

After about fifteen minutes, he heard a team and wagon approaching from his right. As the driver approached, he could see Bass crouching there with his rifle in his hand, and a puzzled look came to the driver's face. He started to pull the wagon to a stop, but Bass motioned for him to go on.

It was Bass' good fortune that the driver was Josh Leadingfox, and they had known each other for several years. In fact, Josh had served as a posse man for Bass on a few occasions.

Josh cast a knowing eye in Bass' direction as he slapped his reins on the team, and they returned to their usual pace.

When the wagon got to a point where Bass was sure it was between him and the walk-way, where the man with the shotgun had entered, Bass rushed across the street and slipped into the walkway between the funeral home and the black-smith's shop. He hurried to the back of the store and cautiously looked around the corner.

The area was clear, and he moved in a crouched position quickly to the other side of the funeral home. He crouched even lower and looked around the edge of the building into the occupied walkway.

Just as Bass had suspected, the man he was looking for was there. He was standing deep enough into the walkway that he could not be seen from the street, but he was able to see the front of Bass' house.

Bass switched his rifle to his left hand and let it hang at his side. He stood up and entered the walkway. He took a few steps forward, now standing within twenty feet of the man with the shotgun.

"You lookin' for me?" Bass asked.

The man had been somewhat crouched, but the sound of Bass' voice frightened him, and he jumped upright. He started to turn to his left with the shotgun pointed up in the air in his right hand.

Bass said, "Don't move or you're gonna be restin' next door."

The warning clearly did not impress the man, and he continued to wheel toward Bass, swinging the shotgun around and lowering it at the same time.

Bass drew and fired. His shot hit the bushwhacker in the right shoulder, causing him to lower the barrel of the weapon of death and pull the trigger at the same time. The blast hit the wall of the general store, ripping loose huge chunks of boards, and propelling them into the air.

The man's shotgun fell to the ground as he grasped his shoulder and leaned forward in pain, nearly dropping to his knees.

Bass rushed forward and grabbed the man's pistol from his holster, and, in the same movement, pushed him from his hiding place out into the street.

He had barely cleared the building when a voice came from across the street. "Tom, you get also 'im?"

"No, he got me," was the reply.

Bass directed the man, "Tell him to get out here and give up now, or I'll put one in 'im. I don't take kindly to bushwhackers."

The man, still clutching his arm, said, "Larry, yah had better get out here. If you don't, he says he's gonna kill yah."

There was silence. Then the man said, "Don't think so. I ain't goin' back to no lockup, and I've waited too long to kill that bastard. I'll take my chances and see who gets who."

Bass told his prisoner, "Set down right there on the boardwalk and don't move. Sounds like I've a little problem here. If you move, I'll finish the job."

The man quickly sat down and hunched over, still nursing his shoulder. He was sitting on the boardwalk with his feet on the ground and his back toward Bass.

Bass rested his Winchester against the side of the building and concentrated on the spot from where the voice had come.

In a very short time, the barrel of a rifle appeared, and a head peered around the corner.

Bass took a breath and squeezed the trigger.

A blood curdling scream came from the other side of the street, followed by, "You, bastard, you missed me. You shot my ear off, but you missed me!"

Bass said, "I was aimin' at your ear. I'd call that a good shot. Now, the next one I'll be aimin' between your eyes."

Bass checked his first prisoner, who was still sitting as instructed, rocking back and forth in pain and slowly lifting his head toward where his partner was concealed.

Bass said, "I've waited long enough. If I come for you, there is only gonna be a short trip for what is left of you. They say that the man who runs this funeral home does a good job. I don't think you want a find out if that's true."

There were several moments of silence, and Bass started wondering if his prey was making a move to try to change his position for a better shot.

Then a cracking voice came from the side of the building. It sounded like it was in great pain.

"Tom, I'm sorry, but we ain't goin' back!"

Tom lifted his head, stared across the street and said, "Larry, I understand. It's OK. You gotta do what you gotta do."

Within seconds, a rifle cracked and the man sitting on the boardwalk clutched his chest and fell forward, into the dirt and muck of the street.

Bass was shocked. He stared at the fallen man as he lay motionless. He could not believe what had just happened. He tried to gather his thoughts and figure what his next move should be.

The answer came quicker than he had expected when a muffled shot came from the side of the building across the street.

Bass ran across the street and placed his back against the wall of the store. He stood for a minute, and then slowly worked his way toward the corner. He stopped and listened, but there was no sound. He took his hat from his head and tossed it into the opening between the buildings, and there was no response. With his pistol in his hand, he slowly rounded the corner. There on the ground was Larry with a hole in his head and blood spattered on the wall behind him.

Of all the things that Bass had witnessed in his life, he had never seen a thing like this. As he was standing there, Josh walked up accompanied by the telegraph runner and several other people. Josh said, "Well, you got 'em. That's a couple more that 'ill go in your book."

Bass shook his head. "I didn't get 'em. They got themselves."

Bass picked his hat up and carefully brushed it off. He put it on, straightened it, then walked across the street and bought the things he needed for the trip.

***

On his trip to Paris, he ran into Deputy Marshal Bud Ledbetter, and they rode together.

Bud said, "I would a thought that you was ahead of me. But it sure is good to see you again and have someone to share the trip."

Bass said, "Do you know what this call for all of us to come to Paris is all about? All my message said was for me to get there, that there was some sort of big problem about a riot, and that I was to be careful on the way."

"No, I don't. But if Dickinson wants us there, it sure must be a big problem. I guess we'll find out when we get there."

They visited about their work, and Bass could not help but tell him of the events that he had just witnessed.

Ledbetter said, "Never had that happen either. Just sounds like they had had all the gray walls they were goin' to have, and this was the only way out."

As they continued, Ledbetter said, "Bass, I'll never forget the time that me and my posse had that no good murderin' skunk holed up in his house, and we had fought him the whole day. I finally got tired of the mess and saw it was gonna go on into the night. I sent for you, and you got there just before sundown. Just a little after you arrived, we had all figured the fightin' was over for the night, but the fool broke cover and ran. My guys laid down a hell of a bunch of shots and just couldn't seem to hit the bastard. You was just standin' there, and I said for you to take him down. You just said that you were gonna break his neck. He was at least a quarter a mile from use. I thought you were just out of your mind. You lifted that old Winchester and fired. He dropped like he had been hit with a brick, and when we got there, you'd done just what you said you were gonna do. I still to this day can't believe the shot. With the near darkness and the distance, it must have been the greatest shot I've ever seen."

Bass looked at Bud and said, "Well, you said you wanted 'im, and I figured you were serious, so I got 'im. Might of been luck, but that was sure what I was aimin' at."

***

The trip continued at as fast a pace as they thought they could sustain, and to their surprise, when they reached the ferry, there were two other marshals waiting for the crossing.

"My God, there must be some real trouble a brewin' if Dickinson wants all of us there." Bud continued, "I would of thought that Bass was enough to put down any trouble that might been a comein'."

The group chuckled, and Bass seemed to take the compliment as just a way of passing time.

The ferry finally arrived, and the boatman said, "Lordy, Lordy, I ain't seen so many stars since I was told about the Milky Way. What in the hell are all you fellers doin'?"

Bud said, "Have no idea. Figured you could tell us somethin'. You mean there has been more of us come by here?"

"Well, just this mornin' I've took at least ten of you lawmen across, and Wilber said he took several yesterday evenin'. I just figured it might have somethin' to do with all those nigger problems they is havin' in Paris."

The boatman immediately looked like he had seen a ghost, when he turned around and saw Bass setting astride his great white stallion.

Bass sat for a moment, then said, "Well, it might be that they is havin' some problems with a bunch of white folks messin' with a bunch of Negro folks."

The boatman quickly responded, "I'll bet you're right. I'll bet your dead right."

The man immediately went to work loading the marshals on the ferry and never let his eyes come even in the area where Bass was standing.

**

When the four marshals entered the town, it was as if a storm was coming. Those few on the street were rapidly rushing to their destination. There were no people standing and visiting, like the common practice. The streets just seemed to be withholding a secret and not wanting to share whatever was consuming the town.

The four rode directly to Marshal Dickinson's office in hopes of some direction and clarification.

The marshal was setting at his desk and looked up as they entered. He quickly rose to his feet and extended his hand to each and every one of the men.

"I'm really glad you fellers made it. We have a really touchy problem here, and I don't aim for it to get out a hand. Have a seat, and, if you like, have some coffee. It was just brewed. It seems as though this place is about to go up like a keg of dynamite. The past few weeks have been very unsettlin'.

"A while back a feller named John Ashley shot and killed a Negro neighbor named Jarrett over some kind of problem, and right after that, Ashley's stock started dying. Then the next thing that happened was his house got burned. His friends and neighbors were convinced that Jarrett's family was responsible. All of a sudden there was a slew of hangin's out by Little Sandy Creek.

"Negro farmer after Negro farmer was strung up, and this whole place was nothin' but a blood bath. Sheriff Gunn knew this thing was out of control, and he told all the blacks that they had better get out of the area, and most of 'em did.

"Then he decided that to calm things down, he would arrest several Negroes and charge them with burnin' down Ashley's house. He tells me he did that so the people would calm down and see that he was tryin' to bring back some kind of law and order.

"He put 'em in jail and hoped that would solve things.

"Our problem is that I've got a bunch of federal prisoners in that jail, and if they make a run on it, I fear that they won't stop with the Negroes. And, by the way, there are some Negro federal prisoners in there. I'm afraid a mob just may clean the place out and have one massive hangin', or maybe burn the jail down."

"I've already got several marshals over there, but I want to make sure that nothin' happens to those people. They are in my care, and I'm responsible for 'em."

Bass stood from his chair, still holding his cup of coffee, and said, "I was raised in this county, but I don't know where Little Sandy Creek is. If you will let Bud and me go there and show some force, that the Marshal service is not about to put up with hangin's, it might help cause the people to stop and think."

Dickinson turned to Bud and said, "Do you think that is a good idea?"

Bud looked first at Bass and then at Dickinson. "If Bass wants to go, and you approve, I'll sure go with him. I don't know if it will help, but a show of force sure seems to calm a lot of situations."

Dickinson thought for a minute, and then said, "You know, I think I'll just let you go, but I'm sendin' two other deputies with you. If we're gonna make a show of force, we should do it right, and I am goin' to leave ten deputies at the jail and put the others on patrol in pairs on all the streets in town. If we can calm 'em down now it probably will keep somethin' major from happin'."

The four deputies got directions to the Little Sandy Creek area and headed there that afternoon. At nearly every stop they made, they found humble farm houses abandoned. Some of them had already been burnt to the ground.

At one stop, a Negro lady came onto her porch with a shotgun in her hand.

Bass made sure she could see the star on his vest, and he left the others at the gate. He rode to the house and tipped his hat as he approached.

"Miss, I am U.S. Deputy Marshal Bass Reeves, and we are just makin' rounds to all the Negro farms, tryin' to let you folks know that we are tryin' to provide some protection to those that have stayed, and that we are wantin' this thing to calm down."

The lady slowly lowered the shotgun, her faced covered with a look of surprise and wonderment. She stared at Bass for a few minutes, and then said, "Did you say you were Bass Reeves?"

"Yes."

"Good God almighty! I have heard stories of you for years. I'm Sarah. My paw was Ned from the Reeves' place."

Bass immediately dismounted and led Lightnin' to the house.

"What a surprise. I never had any idea what had become of your pa. I knew that Master Reeves had died, and that Nancy had moved away, but never thought that Ned would still be around here."

"Well, Paw passed a few years ago, but he talked a lot about you and your mama. He told stories to me, and then he told stories to my kids. He just couldn't seem to quit talkin' about those times. I would've never believed that I would've met you. I am so glad I've been blessed this way."

"I don't know what a blessin' it was, but it is sure a pleasure to meet you, and I'm so sorry to hear about Ned. You know he was about as close as anyone to a father to me."

Sarah said, "Can you stay a while?"

"No, I got to get back on the rounds with the others. What are you plannin' to do?"

"Oh, we is a leavin'. We is just too scared to stay here. They hung my uncle, and all the men in the area has already gone. We is just packin' up some things, and we'll be out of here."

"Probably a right smart thing to do."

"Tell me about your mama. Has she passed?"

"No, she is still alive and kickin'. One tough woman, and for your information she speaks from time to time about your pa and the others she left behind."

"Well, Lordy be. Tell her you seen me, and tell her she is like a family member, from all the stories I've heard."

"I sure am sorry for all your troubles and hope things work out for you." Bass tipped his hat and rode back to the gate, slowly shaking his head as he went.

As he approached the group of fellow deputy marshals, he said, "Boys, you just won't believe that a part of my life just jumped up in my face. Just goes to show you never know when or where things will appear.

***

The patrols appeared to work, and over the next few days, things slowly changed back to normal. In a few weeks, all of the marshals returned to their assigned location, and Bass was more than happy that he was back in the hunt and on the job.

Chapter 18

Story

Bass decided to stop by Ed Young's place for a visit. Ed had proven not only to be a friend, but he also was a great source of information on the happenings in the area. He had proven most helpful in their search for the killers of Sam Sixkiller, and Bass felt that he should at least give him some credit.

As Bass entered the homestead, Ed came out on the porch with an uncommon look of concern on his face.

"Bass, I should've known that you would show up."

"Why's that Ed?"

"Well, it seems of late that you show up shortly after something dreadful happens at my place. You and Ben came by after I got my guns and horse stole, and thanks to you, Ben brought those back, no worse for the wear. But I not only got my ridin' horse took the other night, but they got my new team. I'd just bought 'em and had a contract to haul freight. Now I'm out the money, and probably I'll lose the contract. I just got back about an hour ago from walkin' to town to report it. I wouldn't even have been here if I hadn't caught a ride back."

"They got your team and ridin' horse just the other day? You see 'em or know who did it?"

"Hell no! They was slick as axel grease. I never heard a sound, and all I know is that when I went to get some eggs in the mornin', they was gone. I had hoped that it wouldn't happen to me, and sure should've been more careful, 'cause I've had two neighbors lose horses in the last week. Damn, that sure makes me mad. In fact, everyone in the area is hoppin' mad that this stuff just keeps a happenin'."

"Well, let me take a look and see if I can find some signs. I'm sure sorry for your loss, and I promise I'll try to see what is goin' on and put a stop to it."

As they walked to the corral, Bass said, "I just stopped by to be friendly and to thank you for your help on that Sixkiller murder. I'm sorry that it's turned into a hardship for you."

"Oh hell, I'm glad you stopped. I'm sorry that it's turned into a job for you."

Bass looked around and checked for signs. He was able to find boot prints that led off into a row of trees that was about five hundred yards from the house. Here he lifted up a wooden bucket and said, "Is this yours? Looks like the reason you didn't hear 'em is they took a full bucket of grain and led the horses here, before they put 'em in their string. Look at all the tracks. There was at least ten unmanned horses and four or five riders. Looks like a real gang operation. The only gang this size I know of is the Tom Story bunch. They been comin' and goin' for years now, and they is real slick at it. Got it down to a fine art. However, this is the closest I've been to 'em, and I see no way they're gonna be able to get away pullin' that many horses."

Ed said, "Well, that eases my mind a little, knowin' that you think you can catch 'em before they get rid of my horses."

"Let's go to the house, and you draw me a picture of the brands on 'em, and I'll try my best to get 'em back for you."

Bass took the paper and picked up the trail. He could tell by the tracks that they were moving much faster than he had expected. It was evident that they knew the trail and now were moving with but one purpose, and that was to get to the Texas border and hopefully to safety. Bass decided to cut across country and try to intercept them before they got that accomplished.

He had heard that Story and his bunch had a hideout somewhere in the Chickasaw Nation and close to the Red River. With this in mind, he headed toward Tishomingo. The trip was challenging, but he knew that if he could get there, he had people who knew the Nation and hopefully would give him a clue as to where he might encounter the gang.

As he approached Cherokee Town, he was stopped by a Chickasaw Freedman named Jim Bright. They had previously met when Bass was in the Territory looking for whiskey runners, and Jim had been a reliable source of information.

"Jim, what has been happenin' with you?"

"Bass, I'm so glad that you came along. There is a lot of trouble brewin', and we gotta have some relief. There's a bastard that those damned Texas cowmen have brought into the country, and he is a killin' the Chickasaw 'cause they is a raisin' hell about all the cows brought across the river to eat our grass. He don't fight fair. He has bushwhacked several tribesmen, and he jest seems to know where they are, and when he can strike. We need your help bad. Can you do somethin' about it?"

"Jim, I'm after a bunch they call the Story gang, and they are pullin' a big string of stole horses. I hear your problem, and I'll try to put a stop to it, but do you know anythin' about this bunch?"

"I think I know somethin' that might help and glad to do it, but you gotta promise to get rid of the bastard that is a doin' so much killin'."

"What do you know?"

"I was down on the river fishin', and I ran across a really good setup camp right on the banks. It had about four tents and a huge corral, much bigger than should be needed for that size of camp. If I was a bettin' man, I'd guess it was built to hold horses till they had 'nough to make a crossin' into Texas."

"Jim, sounds like jest the thing I'm lookin' for. Now, you got any idea where this bushwhacker is a holed up? I really need to catch these horse thieves, but a man doin' murder has to come first."

"I'll tell you what I'll do. If you'll go after him, I'll go with you, and then I'll take you right to where I seen the camp."

"Sounds fair 'nough. You know what this man looks like? You totin' any iron? If you are, I'll make you my posse man."

"Sure do know 'em, and I got my pistol in my saddle-bag, and I can strap it on."

Bass reached into his other boot and pulled out his shotgun and handed it to Jim. "This won't do much good if we get in a fight of any distance, but if we get on 'em, it sure could make a difference. Let's get on the hunt."

Jim led the way, and they backtracked some of the trail that Bass had already traveled. They had not gone more than two miles when Jim motioned for Bass to halt. He leaned over in the saddle and spoke softly. "Right up in front of us is a spot in the road where he walloped two men. I think we should be careful from here."

Bass asked, "Why don't we just tie up here and scout on foot? If I was layin' in wait for someone, I'd pick them trees on that hill over there on the right. Why don't you circle around to the right side, and I'll kinda go straight at it from here. I'll give you five minutes to get in place before I start movin'. Be careful. If he's there and the man you think he is, he'll kill you just for snoopin'."

"I'll do that. I think I can get right close in that time. I ain't afraid."

Bass squatted down and pulled his watch out. All the time, he was concentrating on the trees that provided such a great concealment for anyone with murder on his mind. He felt certain he saw movement, and his alertness heightened.

When he was sure that he had given Jim enough time, he started to work his way directly toward his objective.

Due to the terrain, he was having trouble keeping from being spotted, but he knew that he had to make this move and deal with whatever happened.

He had gone only about fifty feet when he heard a rifle crack. The next thing he knew, his head was bare. His big broad brimmed hat hit the ground before he could. He trained his rifle on the spot from where he had seen smoke come and hoped that the fool would raise up just enough for him to return the favor.

Before he had the opportunity, another rifle crack pierced the air. This was followed immediately by the roar of Bass' shotgun, signaling that Jim was on the job.

Bass now knew that the bushwhacker was occupied, so he moved with great speed to close the distance. He heard no more shots, and while he kept in as crouched a position as possible, he still worked his way up the rise.

As he got closer, he slowed and kept his Winchester at the ready. No sounds came from the clump of trees, as he continued on his journey. He finally got to a position where he could take shelter behind a rock. He waited, and still no sound came from the hiding place.

Bass shouted, "Jim, you alright?"

There was no reply. "Jim, you alright?"

The same silence was the only reply he got.

After a few moments, Bass raised his bare head. It drew no fire and no response.

Bass got to his feet and slowly finished the fifty foot trip to the trees, all the while with his Winchester at the ready.

Even before he got to where he could see the hiding area, he knew there was not going to be any fight coming from the man hidden there.

In a tree about eight feet off the ground hung a part of a vest that was covered with blood. It hung there as if it had been nailed there with a ten penny nail. The vest slowly turned in the wind.

Bass straightened up and walked the remaining distance.

The sight that greeted him was nearly what he had anticipated. On the ground was what was left of the bushwhacker. His chest was blown open and part of his insides was oozing from the gigantic hole in his body.

Bass turned from him to see Jim lying on his back with his hands clutching his stomach. He rushed to him and got there just as Jim's grimace slowly relaxed and he tried to utter his last words.

Bass lifted his friend's head and saw the stain from the blood that had escaped from his mouth. Bass carefully and respectfully pulled Jim's eyelids down.

With both bodies strapped to their horses, Bass took the two men back to town. He delivered the bodies to the funeral home and went directly to the telegraph office.

He sent a message to the marshal's office in Paris. "Two men dead. Stop. One posse man, Jim Bright. Stop. One bushwhacker unknown. Stop."

Bass then went to his horse and tried to straighten his hat. It sure didn't feel right with a part of the brim gone. He felt naked without his proper hat that had been an important part of his dress for so many years. But, he had to get back on the trail of the horse thieves, and without the information he had hoped that Jim would have provided.

The Red River runs the full length of the state, but he knew that Jim would not have been far from the middle of the Chickasaw Nation, so he headed due south.

As he got close to the river, he stopped every person he encountered and asked if they knew of an encampment that had a large corral. It was not until two days later that he hit pay dirt.

With his new directions, he rapidly moved toward his target. But, when he got there, the site was totally empty of people and horses. He went to the corral and could see that he had missed the gang by at least a day. The signs were clear that a fresh group of horses had been in the corral, but had been removed and probably forded across the river to the Texas side.

He crossed the river, but it was impossible to pick up the trail due to all the traffic that had crossed after they had. He decided to return to Paris and give a report. He hoped that when he got there, he could get some leads from other marshals.

It only took a hard day's ride to reach Paris, but his entry still forced him to go back in time and relive his early days as a slave. . He recalled thinking that this was the center of the world and that there surely could not be any place larger or more modern. He recalled how he had loved to accompany Master Reeves and the close call he had had when he shot the man trying to molest Miss Nancy. It just seemed like yesterday, but he quickly returned to reality.

Bass shook his head, realizing how his life had changed. The thoughts were soon cleared from his mind as he got closer to the marshal's office.

When he entered, he was greeted by the clerk who said, "Got your message about the killin's. Who was Jim Bright?"

Bass took off his hat, with the missing front quarter of the brim, and slapped it on his knee. "He was a Chickasaw Freedman who had volunteered to help me stop a murder and find some horse thieves. He paid with his life for tryin' to be what all citizens should be. I swore him in so that anythin' he did would be legal and tight. I was just sorry he couldn't come away on two feet, but he got the bastard that killed him."

"Well, just make sure you get it in your report."

"I'm on the trail of that slippery Story gang. Nearly got 'em, but was delayed by the killin' of Jim. You got any word on those guys?"

The clerk reached into the pile of papers on his desk, eyeing each as he laid it in another pile. "There was a guy in here this mornin' name of Delaney. Here it is." He picked up a paper. "George Delany. Said he had some fine horses and mules taken from his place and had found out that Tom Story's bunch had done it. Said he would give a nice reward if we could catch 'em, and get his property back. Said if someone wanted to come to his house, he would give 'im all the information. We didn't have a marshal in at the time, but looks like you're here now, and he is ready for some relief."

"Where does this feller live?"

"'Bout two miles south of town you will come to the Hostetler's place, and then you go 'bout four miles to the east. He said you could ask anyone in the area where he lives, if you have any problems."

"I'm headed that way now. I'll send you a telegraph if I hit the trail from there. If not, I'll be back this evenin'."

The directions were good, and Bass moved with great haste. All he could think about was that he had failed Ed, and he sure didn't like that hanging over his head.

Mr. Delaney met Bass as he was riding into the yard. He had a half smile on his face when he saw the badge, but at the same time exhibited anxiousness in his steps.

The man approached hesitantly, but it was apparent that he was pleased that he might get some assistance with his problem. He appeared confused and concerned, while at the same time it was obvious that he wanted some help from the law.

Finally he said, "Take your horse over to the trough and come on up on the porch, and I'll tell you what I know."

Bass complied quickly. He was anxious to get any lead that he could on this bunch that now had become an embarrassment to him.

Delaney pointed to a rocking chair and pulled one up close to Bass. He seemed to realize that if he wanted help, he was going to have to take whatever was sent.

"I had my horses and mules stole and just couldn't stand by and let that happen. I started makin' the rounds of places that I thought I might get a lead and ended up in a saloon in Quiteman. I ran into a friend of mine, I know there, and he told me that he had seen and had had some drinks with a guy by the name of Kinch West. They had rode together with Quantrill years back. Anyway, he and the feller had several drinks for old time sakes and ended up rehashin' their past adventures. As the night went on and the drinks started to take over, this feller said that he was ridin' with a man named Tom Story, and that they were doin' real well stealin' horses in Indian Territory and bringin' 'em down this way and sellin' 'em. As the night wore on, he said they had spotted a string down here and had some buyers up in the Territory that were lookin' for exactly what they had found.

"My horses were as fine a workin' team as there is anywhere, and I had three teams of mules that I had been offered five hundred dollars each for. There weren't anything ordinary about my stock. I got three hundred acres of cotton land, and them teams was what made this place go.

"In this night's story, he said that they had to deliver the stock by yesterday, and that they were goin' to split the money amongst the group and take some time off. He and Story were comin' back here, and he wanted to know if my friend knew some lady that he could spend some time with.

"That is why I am so anxious to get someone on their trail. In fact, if someone knew where they was a crossin', I'd be glad to go along and help. I done my share of fightin' over the years and am hankerin' to first get what is mine back, and second, put a rope around those thievin' bastard's necks."

Bass looked at the ground and rocked back in the chair. "I think I know where they'll cross the river, and if you think they delivered your stock yesterday, then we got no time to waste. If you want to come, go get your gear. I'm packed and have about as strong a hankerin' to get these fellers as you do."

George immediately stood and shouted into the house, "Matilda, get me some grub packed and pack me some clothes! I'm goin' after my stock. Marshal, if you'll wait here, I'll go saddle up and get a pack horse and some campin' stuff."

In an impressively short time, George was back from the barn and ready to go. When Matilda stepped through the door with the bed-roll and a saddlebag full of food, she stopped in mid-stride.

"Who you goin' with?"

"This marshal right here."

She dropped both the bedroll and saddlebags to her sides and just stared.

"Matilda, give me that stuff. I gotta take what help I can get. Without the stock, the bank will have this place in a short time."

She lifted the supplies to him, but the look of displeasure on her face was evident.

After she had placed the supplies into George's hands, she said, "George, I sure hope you know what you is a doin'?" Then she turned and looked at Bass from head to toe. She shook her head from side to side and entered the house.

They headed toward the crossing near the camp-site that Bass had located earlier. Bass walked the site and said, "From what I see, they ain't been here, and that's a good sign. The only thing I know to do is just wait for 'em to come back through. They will have already sold your horses, but if we take 'em, I'd bet we can make 'em tell where and to who they sold 'em. If that happens, I'll go with you and help you get 'em back."

Delaney kicked his boot in the dirt. "I really hate to just set here. I want my stock back."

"I know, but where we start a lookin' is a mystery, and if we leave here, we'll probably miss 'em. It is a big gamble for us to go lookin' when we know they'll be back. So my advice is that we just wait."

They pitched a camp up the trail from the horse thieves 'holed up and waited. To pass time, they fished in the Red River. This diversion brought back many memories for Bass. He recalled the times he had fished at the Reeves' place and the few times he had taken his boys to fish. He thought about all the times he should have been with his family rather than on the trail of some no good.

By day three, Delaney was fit to be tied. He started to show more and more signs of disgust that nothing was happening. There had been several passersby to the ford, but they never were the ones he wanted so badly.

On the third day, things changed. Bass and George had developed a friendship from their continual contact. George had nearly forgotten the color of Bass' skin. He had seen the strong dedicated man that Bass was, and the longer he was around him, the more he respected him.

As they sat in front of their tent, they heard the approach of several sets of hooves. They did not jump to attention, as this had happened several times before. But from their location, they could see up the road, and when the riders appeared, George jumped to his feet.

"That's my mules! That's my mules!" he said, trying to keep his voice low, but showing great excitement.

Bass rose from the stump he was occupying and casually walked to the well worn trail.

As the two riders approached, Bass stepped into the middle of the trail and held up his hand.

The riders were leading two fine mules, and the group pulled to a halt.

Bass calmly said, "Fellers, I'm Deputy U.S. Marshal Bass Reeves, and I think you have somethin' that belongs to a friend of mine."

One of the men said, "Well, your friend must be some kind of a two bit liar 'cause these mules are mine."

Bass said, "How'd you know I was a talkin' about the mules? I simply said that you had somethin'."

The man replied, "Jest figured."

"Well, since you brought it up, can you show me some papers on those critters?"

"No, I can't and don't aim to."

"Then I would advise you to get down, and let my friend take a look at 'em."

The man sat in his saddle for a moment and started to adjust his seating position. He now was getting the look of a man who was going to defy Bass' command' and Bass knew it. He had seen the look, the movement and expression on a man's face too many times.

Bass said, "You make me think you are about to commit suicide. And I only think it is fair to warn you that you should rethink what you're 'bout to do."

The man again shifted in his saddle and a serious smile started to creep across his face.

Bass said, "I've warned you, and I've ask you nice to step down. From now on, your life is in my hands."

The man was not convinced. He reached for his pistol.

He was far too slow. By the time he had half cleared his holster; Bass had cleared his right Colt and put a bullet in his chest. The man first released his pistol and grabbed his chest. He sat for a moment in the saddle, but his horse was now spooked and ran out from under him.

The man hit the ground with a thud and rolled onto his back.

While this was happening, Bass swung his pistol toward the other rider.

"There is a lot of room here on the ground. If you want to join your partner, just keep on sneaking' toward your pistol."

The man immediately put both hands in the air and said, "No, no, I don't want no part of it."

"Then pull your pistol with two fingers and hand it easy to Mr. Delaney." Which the man readily did.

"Now that that is done, I need a few things from you," Bass said. "What is your name and the name of this fool lyin' here at my feet?"

"That is Tom Story, and I'm Kinch West."

"Where did you sell the rest of the stock that you took from Mr. Delaney?"

"Up by Tishomingo."

"Do you know who and on what farm they went?"

"I don't think I am tellin' you nothin' more."

"Well, suit yourself. Get down off your horse and put your hands behind your back."

Bass secured his hands and then stepped in front of him.

"Let me introduce Mr. Delaney to you. This is the feller you took these mules from. He wants 'em back real bad and he has promised to hang the bastards that took 'em if he don't get 'em back.

"Now you know I can't allow that. By law you have got to get a fair trial. However, I can understand this man's anger. So here is what I'm gonna do. I'm gonna turn my back and walk to my horse. I am gonna ride back to Paris and tell 'em that I left you here in Mr. Delaney's good care.

"The only way that I will interrupt my journey is if you start talkin' right now and not only tell Mr. Delaney where the rest of his stock is, but where and to who you sold that string you stole from up around Muskogee a while back.

"Since you is on the ground, and Mr. Delaney is not a big man. I'd think if he had any idea of hangin' you, he'd just have to throw the rope over that there limb and pull you up slow.

"I sure hope he don't want to do that 'cause that is sure one terrible way to die. I saw one feller get that done to him, and the first thing he did was make some really awful sounds, and as his feet left the ground, he really kicked his feet somethin' terrible, must have been in some kind of pain. The next thing he did was piss his pants, really a disgustin' sight. The last thing I recall was his eyes seemed to be wantin' to jump out of his head and his tongue stuck so far out of his mouth that it scared me, thought that maybe his guts was gonna follow. They didn't though, but it really turned a wild shade of blue or maybe it was purple.

"Now, I gotta get Mr. Tom Story loaded on his horse and take him to Paris. Can't have the likes of him clutterin' up the road. By the way, Mr. Delaney, if you should happen to hang this Mr. Kinch, please don't leave him hangin' for long. They start to stink real bad, and the crows come along and pick at the eyes. Really unsightly. Please, cut him down and cover him up."

Bass turned and walked to get Story's horse. He then led the horse to the camp, saddled Lightnin' and returned to where Story was laying. Bass struggled, but finally got Story over his saddle and secured.

While he was doing this, Delaney walked to his saddle and retrieved his lariat. He slowly returned to his position near the secured bandit and stood directly in from of him, lightly slapping the lariat against the side of his leg. As he did this, a smile crossed his face.

Bass pulled himself into his saddle and turned toward the two men. Kinch had a look of fear in his eyes. He finally said, "Mister, mister, take me with you. I don't want a be here with this feller. I think it's your job to take me, and I demand that you do!"

"Well, I sure would like to, but I can't keep my eye on you and drag this horse all at one time. I'll be back tomorrow and get you. Mr. Delaney will take good care of you while I am gone."

"Wait, I'll tell you all you want to know right now. Just don't leave me here with him. The horses that we got in Muskogee were sold to a guy named Jenner near Gilmer, and the horses that goes to this man is up by Tishomingo, just like you was told, the man who has 'em is named Josh Whitcome, and I know where he lives. Now get this man away from me."

Bass smiled and said, "All I'm gonna do is help him get you back in the saddle. Then you're comin' with us to help get his stock back."

They immediately broke camp and headed toward Tishomingo. When they got there, Bass had them take a side street to the telegraph office where he sent a message that read, "Tom Story dead. Stop. Retrieved some mules. Stop. Going to Gilmer for more. Stop"

The negotiation for the return of Mr. Delaney's stock was swift and smooth, as Bass had removed the money from Story's body and took the rest from Kinch.

Mr. Delaney was delighted with the outcome and handed Bass one hundred dollars. The three pulled the string back to Delaney's house, and he let the captive and Bass spend the night in the barn.

The next morning, Mrs. Delaney brought them a huge breakfast of eggs and sausage with some of the best biscuits that Bass had had in a long time. She stood for some time, and then pulled herself up to a full upright position and displayed as much composure as she could muster, and said, "Thank you, but I woulda never had believed it." Then turned and went to the house.

The trip to Gilmer was long, but not difficult. However, the negotiation with Mr. Jenner was not that easy. He said, "I paid good money for these horses, and I ain't givein' 'em up."

Bass ended up showing him the brands and description of the horses, and said, "I am sorry for your problems, but you never asked them for proof of ownership, and you took your chances with the purchase. Now you can give me the horses, and I'll give you this hundred and thirty dollars that is left of the money I took from the thieves, or you can face a charge of receivin' stolen property. There's no way you'll win that, and you're gonna lose the horses either way."

Reluctantly, Jenner let Bass take the horses.

Bass drug Kinch all the way to Muskogee, where he returned the horses to Ed Young. When that was done, Bass took Kinch to the Indian Police. They said, "This guy is a white man, and we can't deal with 'im."

Bass said, "If you look real close, you'll see that he is like a pregnant squaw and has a little Indian in 'im. That gives you the right to take 'im to court and do with 'im what you do to Indians who steal horses."

As he turned to leave, he said, "This man and the feller I killed have stole more horses than any bunch I know. I hope that you take that in to consideration when he gets to court. I think I know what the verdict will be, and I hope you carry it out to the fullest extent. It will make the Territory a better place."

Chapter 19

Defeat

Bass approached the establishment in his usual cautious way. He had learned over the years that it was impossible to judge what were common ordinary days and days full of violence.

He tied Lightnin' to the hitch and stepped onto the porch. He peered through the window to assess the inhabitants. This turned out to be a poor choice because he was immediately recognized by a desperado by the name of Hellabee Sammy who had avoided him for years.

Bass could hear the crashing of glass and the sound of tables being turned over as the fleeing man rushed to the backdoor. Just as Bass entered, he was greeted by the roar of a pistol and the explosion of the doorsill. He lifted his pistol just as the escaping suspect disappeared out the back door.

Bass rushed toward the back but was delayed by the strewn tables and chairs that he had to negotiate. When he made it to the door, he carefully stepped out into the blazing sunlight in time to see his prey's huge black stallion turn the corner of the building in full stride.

Bass did not hesitate. He turned back into the building and retraced his steps back out the front door. He jumped into the saddle and pulled Lightnin's head toward the escaping fugitive. He slapped his reins on Lightnin's rump, and the race was on.

Bass know he had a great horse under him, and the run should not be challenging. He leaned into the saddle and again applied the reins to his mount's rump. Now they were clear of town, and Bass could see his target applying the whip to the big black stallion.

The rider evidently knew the country and headed for a large outcropping of trees. He guided his mount with great skill through the trees and then descended into a wide, open valley. Here, he repeatedly applied his whip, and the black beast responded in amazing style.

Bass was impressed, but knew that his horse was as good as any and all he had to do was keep the wanted man and his horse in sight. He put Lightnin' into a strong pace but refused to go full out. He had seen what the rider and his horse could do, so he decided to let time take its course. Lightnin' was strong and healthy, and Bass knew that time would take its toll.

To Bass's surprise, the distance between the two seemed to get greater. He finally decided that he had to put his stallion in full speed if he had any chance of capturing this maverick.

Bass called for all that Lightnin' had and received it. The big white stallion now laid his ears back and started taking huge strides. They were soon closing the gap on their prey and Bass knew that it was only time until the race would be over. They had been on the chase for nearly thirty minutes, and it was time for some relief for both parties.

When Bass realized that he had nearly conquered his target, he was shocked to see the distance start to grow again.

Bass thought that he might pull up and let his Winchester close the distance, but then had a second thought. This man was not wanted for murder or any major crime, so why should he take the chance of killing him or, worse yet, kill the horse he was riding.

Bass made up his mind that he was not going to overtake this scoundrel and his great horse, so Bass slowed and decided to use his skills as a tracker to make the arrest he was now so determined to accomplish.

The black stallion was soon out of sight, and Bass had a sudden realization that he had lost a race that he had wanted to win. He had never had this happen to him, and he was having problems dealing with it. This made him more determined than ever to track this man if it took him till the next day.

He easily picked up the tracks and put Lightnin' in a walk. After some time, he was amazed the stride of the big stallion had only slightly shortened. He followed the tracks until he topped a ridge and was greeted by the rolling Arkansas River. The tracks stopped at the edge of the water, and his prey disappeared into the unknown.

Bass went nearly a mile up river in hopes of seeing where the rider had left the river and headed back toward his more familiar country, but his effort was to no avail. It was also getting close to nightfall, and he realized that even if he picked up the trail, the dark would soon bring protection for his prey.

Bass sat in the saddle and pushed his big brimmed hat back on his head. He was having difficulty in dealing with the fact that he had been out run and out rode.

He had realized that he was getting older, but for some reason, this chase had brought it home more than anything in the past. He slowly consoled himself by thinking that if he had King, his great old stallion, this would have never happened. Then he grasped the fact that he had just been defeated, and there was no reason to blame anyone or anything with the fact.

He turned Lightnin' and started the long trip back. All the while, he was thinking that it was maybe a good lesson. He had to face the fact that he was not always going to win and that he had won far more than his share of contest. The fact that losing this challenge had not been anything more than an embarrassment gave him some relief.

As he now retraced his steps, he started to relax, but at the same time he also made a vow that if he ever he had a chance to run this rascal down again, he would have a better plan than to simply make a race out of it.

He started back through the trees after clearing the meadow and out from behind a tree stepped an old Indian man with braids hanging down across his thin chest. He had a smile on his face that showed the lack of his front teeth.

"See yah didn't get 'em." He then broke out in a big laugh.

"Hear yah never miss, but yah sure did this time. Don't get all out of sorts over it. I seen that black devil run many a time, and there ain't nothin' they can do 'cept eat his dust.

"Now if yah is as smart as I hear yah is, yah will take a little direction from an old man. Yah know where the dugout is up on Roarin' Creek over by Beggs? If you know it, you can jest go there and set. There's a pretty young gal there that has a real thing for the Hellabee Sammy yah was a chasin'. I don't know if it is the guy or his horse she got a thing for, but she lets 'im hang out there. So if yah jest goes there and sets, yah 'ill get yah man."

Bass thought a minute and then laughed. "I thank you for your advice. If I'd known that earlier, I would of sure saved myself some hard ridin' and a little loss of pride. I think I'll take your tip and just mosey over there. If I take my time, I should get there about the time the feller comes rollin' out of the hay."

Chapter 20

Klu Klux Klan

It was a peaceful morning, and Bass had decided that it would be a great time to get the work he disliked most out of the way. He stopped in the café and had his favorite Sunday morning breakfast. He had not wakened his wife because he knew that she would insist on him going to church, and he knew he had to get this task done.

Bass was sitting at his desk making sure that all the figures he was about to turn in for his last run were accurate and complete. This part of the job had been the part that he hated the most. In his mind, it was much easier to face a man with a gun and a bad attitude than to deal with all of these details.

But he knew that it was a very important part of his job, especially if he wanted to get paid. The door to the office opened briskly, and a young man rushed in. His face was flushed, and he was in a half state of dress. The sweat was streaming from his face so profusely that you would have thought he had poured a bucket of water over his head.

The boy tried to speak, but was so occupied with getting his breath that all he could say was, "My dad, my dad." Then he would return to struggling for breath.

Bass rose and poured a glass of water. He quickly rounded the desk and handed the glass to the muttering boy. "Now, take your time and relax. A few seconds is not gonna change much."

The boy grasped the glass, lifted it to his lips and held it there while he took another breath. He finally took a long drink and fell back into the chair.

Bass said, "Now young man can you tell me what you got on your mind?"

"Yes sir. I ran all the way from Wybark — well nearly all the way. My horse came up lame about half way here."

"Son, that's right good distance. I can understand why you is winded, but what was your hurry?"

"My pa told me to get here quick and get a marshal. Is one here? There's been a bunch of killin out by the house and we need help. My pa will thrash me if I don't get it done.

"Son settle down. I'm a marshal and this sounds serious to me. Do you know who got killed or exactly where they got killed?"

"Yep, know that, and I can show yah, if I can get a ride back."

"Well, I don't have a spare horse, but you can ride with me behind the saddle. You up to that?"

"Mister, my Pa said for me to get some help quick, and if I don't, he would skin me alive, so I am ready for the ride."

"You sure you're up to it? You look pretty tuckered out."

"Mister, if I don't do what my Pa says, there is liable to be another murder for you to look at. So I am ready when you are."

They exited the office and went to the hitching post. Bass untied the big black stallion and walked around to his side. He pulled the cinch tight and made sure the saddle was secure. He then hopped into the saddle and reached his hand down for the boy.

"You sure that he will let us ride double?"

"No doubt. The guy that used to own him had a girl friend that he kept in line by lettin' her ride with 'em.

"I sure hope you're right. He looks like he could be one bad creator if he wanted to be."

"Let's go. Your Pa must be waitin'."

The two traveled the few miles and crossed the river. The boy gave directions from there, and they soon were at the M.K.T. railroad yard. The site of the problem was not hard to determine because of the crowd of people that were mulling around the area.

Bass and the boy dismounted and walked to the crowd. When the crowd separated, Bass was slow to step forward.

Yes, there was a body of a man laying there, and it was evident that it had been there for several hours, but the thing that had stopped Bass was the fact that he was wearing a blood soaked white sheet, and the hood that had been over his head was laying at his side. The hood was completely soaked in blood. It looked evident that he had attempted to stop his bleeding with the hood.

Bass paused for a moment and studied the faces of those in the crowd. He then turned away and looked back across the yard, where there was a trail of blood coming from the north.

Bass turned his gaze back to the crowd and said, "Does anyone here know this man or anything about what happened here?"

This was followed by a deadly silence. So silent that the only noise heard was the chirping of birds in the trees that edged the yard.

At last, a man looked up from the body and said, "That's Jim Mathews. He works here at the yard. I don't know nothin' else about this here crime, but there is two dead people about a mile from here. I already been there, and it is one hell of a sight, especially for a Sunday morning."

"You know those people over there?"

"Sure, most everybody knows Ed Chalmers and Mary Headly. They is good people, but they sure shouldn't of been doin' what they been doin'."

Bass looked at the man for several minutes. He studied his face and, at the same time, glanced at others in the crowd. Bass was hoping to read their faces in response to the man's statement. Most of them dropped their heads at the statement, but a few shook their heads in agreement.

Bass knew Ed and Mary. He knew them pretty well. Ed was not a friend of his, but they had visited on occasion. He was a hard working Negro farmer that had done nothing but work hard and stayed out of trouble. In fact, he had been a source of information on a few of Bass' searches. The information he had given had always been accurate and useful.

Mary was a likeable somewhat pretty blond-headed, white woman. She had always been friendly and kind when Bass had stopped at the small hut she shared with Ed.

The hood and sheet now was making a lot of sense to Bass. The Klan and its sympathizers had become more and more active in the area over the past few years, and that was one reason why Bass and Marshal Bennet had agreed that Bass should limit his work, as much as possible, to Indian and Negro crimes. They had discussed the possible repercussions if he killed a white man or even brought one in that was a member of the Klan.

Bass looked into the crowd and said, "Who would like to make two dollars?"

A voice asked, "What do I have to do?"

"You need to ride into town and get Marshal Bennet, quickly, and tell him I need him now. Tell him I'll be at Ed Chamber's place."

A man stepped forward and said, "For two dollars, I'll do it."

"Then get a goin'," Bass said, as he handed the man two coins.

Bass turned to the other men and said, "Could I get you fellers to help get this body into the shade. It's gonna be a while before Bennet gets here and I want him to have a look at it.

While the movement was being accomplished, Bass did a complete inventory of what evidence he could observe. The most notable was that the corpse had a gun shot that had entered his back and exited his stomach.

Bass felt that it was not possible for him to have gotten this far from the Chamber's place without assistance, due to the severity of his wound.

He turned and traced the blood trail walking very slowly and taking in everything and anything that might be of help. He finally reached a low spot where there had been a small amount of water standing. He could see that the victim had walked through it. He was sure of that, because of the matching prints of the shoes. However, he was able to find another set of prints which were totally different, at least two shoe sizes smaller. Because of the depth of the print, he quickly assumed that the person making them had been carrying more weight than the size of the print normally might indicate as the approximate weight of the owner.

Bass walked to a building on the grounds and found a shovel. He meticulously dug the footprint up and carefully carried it to a safe place where it could set in the sunlight that was now bathing the grounds.

Bass then went back to the stallion and headed toward the Chamber's place. He rode slowly and looked for any possible signs that could shed more light on the happenings of the previous night.

When he got to the house, it was totally vacant. He was shocked that there were not at least a few people there, as murder and crime were what seemed to be a major point of entertainment to the people. It was something that everybody wanted to say that they had seen, or they were there. Such cases were the topic of many conversations, as it was a total break from the usual discussions of the weather and the crops.

When Bass entered the small hut, he understood why there was no one in the area. Even the most curious would not want to be observers of the gruesome sight that was awaiting him. Not since the death of Charley at the Mankiller's house had he seen such carnage. Bass had seen many a ghastly sight, but this was about as stomach-turning as he could remember.

To one side of the small room lay Ed. One side of his face and head was missing. His brains were protruding from their encasement and oozed out onto the dirt floor. The flies had found their source of nourishment and were in a continual state of swarming. They were so numerous that their movement produced a continual buzzing sound that added to the distasteful setting.

The blood on the dirt floor had created a ghastly form of mud, and the smell of death filled the small room. The most disturbing sight of all was that Ed's pants had been slashed from his body. This was evident from the knife wounds showing on what was left of his legs. The murders had cut Ed's private parts from his body and thrown them into the corner of the room.

Bass turned and stepped to the door. He leaned against the casement and stuck his head out into the clear air of the morning. He gasped for air and felt his stomach tighten. Bass actually felt as if he might lose his early morning breakfast. He finally pulled himself together and removed his large bandana from his back pocket, and wiped his forehead and face. He then made a mask with the bandana, hoping that it would filter some of the stink of the room, for he knew that he had to reenter to continue his investigation.

He walked around for a few moments on the outside and looked to the sky. He had no idea what he was looking for — he just wanted to be occupied with something that was natural.

Bass took a deep breath and turned to reenter. He looked across the room and saw the blonde hair of Mary disheveled and spread on the dingy pillow. He approached with caution. He watched where he stepped, not only to avoid the murky mud on the floor, but to make sure that he did not contaminate any clues, that might be in the room.

The same swarm of flies was feasting on her mutilated body. They had especially concentrated on her chest. She had a bullet hole in her forehead, but the main attraction for the scavengers was the area where her breast had been crudely cut from her body. Her face was frozen, displaying agonizing pain.

This caused Bass to wonder if the removal of her breast had come before the shot to her forehead.

"My God, what a display of hate and cruelty and humiliation has been done to these poor people," Bass said out loud.

He did not know why he had said this to an empty room, but the fact that he had seemed to make him feel better.

He turned to the door and again left the unholy place. He went to a wagon that was in the yard and sat down on its tail. The bandana now had better uses, so he removed it and continually wiped his forehead and face.

His wait was short as he heard Marshal Bennet approaching. He turned and stared, having to shade his eyes from the sun, which was to the approaching marshal's back.

"Well, marshal, welcome to the site of one of the worst tragedies I've been to in a long time. I know you're gonna have to go in there, but I advise you that you won't believe what you see. You should put your bandana over your nose. The smell will make you lose your lunch, if the scene doesn't.

"Before you go, let me tell you. They castrated Ed, and they cut Mary's tits off. This information might take some of the shock off."

"Bass, you can't be serious?"

"I'm as serious as anythin' I've ever told you. I didn't want to believe it either, but it is there. It looks like the devil's work."

"I guess I might as well go in." He adjusted his bandana and entered. Bass was sure he heard Bennet gag at least twice before he exited.

Bennet's face was as white as a new pair of longjohns when he exited. He walked to the wagon and sat next to Bass.

"My God, that is the most brutal sight I have ever seen, and I've seen a lot of killin' in my day. What could make people do things like that?"

"Hate is the only reason for that kind of thing," Bass said. "There ain't no other answer. I can only figure that some of 'em folks just had all they could stand of a Negro and a white woman livin' together and decided to make an example out of 'em.

"Well, now, we gotta solve this, and I have one or two good things to go on. Did you see the body at the yards? I got a footprint saved that don't belong to 'im, and the fact that he worked for the railroad makes me believe that some of the people that works with him is involved or knows somethin'."

The pair mounted and started heading back toward the railroad yard. As they rode, they continued to talk about the case.

"Do you know any of the fellers that work there? If you do, do you know one of them that is about five-foot-two and kinda small in size?"

"Let me get to thinkin' here. I know most everybody in this area, and most of the people that work here live in Gibson. You know they don't allow Negroes to live in town, and I understand that several of the stores won't even sell to a Negro, not even food.

"As I remember, there is a feller that works at the yard by the name of Howard Teal that is kind of a runt. I remember when I first met him wonderin' what kind a hand he would make."

Bass said, "You know where he lives?"

"He is like most of the rest. He lives right on the edge of town over at Gibson."

"Let me show you the shoe print that I saved. It should be dry by now."

The men reached the yard, and Bass led the way to the spot behind the fence where he had left the print.

"Have a look at that. I don't think it is much bigger than a woman's shoe, and the wear on the heal and toe tells me that the wearer probably drags his foot."

"By God, I thank you're right. This is a real clue."

Bass smiled and said, "I don't know how good a clue it is, but I think it sure gives us a place to start. Let's take a ride over to Gibson and just drop in on Mr. Teal. Might be real interesting."

They mounted and started the trip to Gibson. They decided to take their time and think about how they were going to handle the visit.

Bass said, "I think one of the things that you should drop on this feller is that Ed was my uncle, and that I am really upset over the whole affair. It will get all over town and might make the culprits uneasy."

Bennet thought for a while and said, "Might work. I hate to change the subject, but that stallion you are a ridin' sure looks familiar. I don't mean no offense, but ain't he the horse they call Nigger?"

"No offense taken, 'cause he is the horse they call Nigger, and he is the fastest thing I have set atop of for some time."

Bennet pushed his hat back on his head and said, "I have seen him run, and I've heard a lot of stories about him."

"One of the stories about him you might have heard is how he outran me and Lightnin' a while back."

"Well, I didn't want to bring that up, but yep, that is one of the stories. How in the hell did you end up with 'im?

"After the chase, I ran into a wise old Indian, and he was gettin' a real kick out of what had happened. Anyway, he gave me a tip on how I could catch Sammy, the guy that was ridin' him.

"One day, I was over by Beggs and just happened to go by the place the Indian had told me about. Sure as shootin', the horse was in the corral, so I went to the house and listened. The noise from inside told me that I had my man in a position where he sure wasn't gonna run. I just walked in the house and pulled my pistol and told Sammy he might as well stop what he was a doin' and come with me. You might say I caught him with his pants down. In fact you could say I caught him with no pants."

Bennet laughed and said, "Well, that tells me how you caught Sammy, but not how you got the horse."

"Sammy had a string of charges against 'im, nothin' too big, but big enough that he needed a good lawyer to get 'im out of his mess. He had no money, and without a lawyer, he was lookin' at probably three or four years.

"You know after my murder trial, I had to sell most of my horses and my farm just to pay the attorney fees, so I was in the market for a good horse, and luckily, I had just collected a five hundred dollar bounty. I offered it to him, and he was in no condition to refuse. That is how I got Nigger, but I'm gonna change his name to Spot."

"Spot? Hell, he's solid black."

"I know, but he's just one big black spot ain't he?"

Bennet let out another laugh and slapped his reins on his horse's rump.

When they approached the Teal house, they pulled themselves together and put on their most serious face.

They dismounted, and Bennet walked to the door and knocked.

Mrs. Teal came to the door, and when she saw that it was the marshal, her face flushed. She tried to smile and look composed, but the more she worked at it, the more evident it was that she was nervous.

"Marshal, what are you doin' here?"

This greeting also told both men that she was highly anxious, as it came out in a high pitch, then suddenly dropped back into a normal tone.

Bennet tipped his hat and asked, "Is Howard here? I'd like to visit with him for a spell. Can I come in?"

Mrs. Teal evidently was caught completely off guard. She stammered as she searched for words and turned a piercing glance toward Bass.

Without thinking she said, "Yes, but that man can't come in my house."

Bennet read the situation perfectly and said, "Oh Lord, I don't want him to come in or even be around white people. Someone killed his uncle, and he is so pissed off that I couldn't be responsible for what he might do, especially to a white lady."

Her face now went completely white. Her eyes got bigger, and she put both hands on her breast, as if she was protecting them from attack.

She then blurted, "Get in here so I can close the door!"

Bennet did as instructed, but turned to Bass and said, "Now, boy, don't go causin' no trouble. These here are respectable white folks."

Bass turned toward the road to conceal the smile that was covering his face. He nearly broke out in laughter, as he realized how shaken the lady was.

While Bennet was in the house, Bass walked around to the back of the house. He could see that a fire had recently been built in the back yard. He slowly walked to the spot, picked up a stick and started to rake through the ashes. At the bottom of the still smoldering fire he found a white strip of what could have been part of a sheet.

Bass quickly fished the smoldering article out with the stick and stomped out all of the glowing embers on its edge. It wasn't a very big piece, but Bass felt that it could serve the purpose he was wanting.

To his great fortune, a rabbit appeared and was casually hopping toward the garden area in the rear of the house. Bass eyed it with great interest. He now had the exact opportunity he had hoped for, but wanted to take his time, so that Bennet could finish whatever questioning he had to do with Howard.

Bass squatted down and waited, all the time eyeing the rabbit that had now entered the garden and had begun doing his shopping for his day's meal.

Bass pulled his watch from his pocket and checked the time. He figured that about another five minutes should be appropriate for what he had in mind.

He rose, went to the woodpile and rummaged through it until he found a piece that was about three feet long and five inches around. He lifted it and felt its heft. This was just right. Bass pulled his knife and removed all the bark from the club. He again lifted it and held it in his extended arm. Perfect.

Now he concluded that the time was right. He drew his Colt and fired. The rabbit went sailing in the air and he rushed to where it had landed. He slit the rabbit open and stuck the end of the club into what was left of the carcass, working it around in order to get as much blood on the end of his mallet as possible. He then lifted the impaled rabbit into the air in order that the blood could run down the instrument as far as possible.

When he was satisfied that he had accomplished his objective he hurled the rabbit into the trees that lay behind the garden.

He then pulled the piece of white cloth from his back pocket and let a small amount of blood drip onto the shabby piece of cloth.

Bass walked back to Spot and worked his mallet down into the boot next to his Winchester. He stood next to his horse waiting for Bennet's return.

As Bennet left the house, he turned and said, "Now, Howard, you understand that I want you and Ed Burns in my office tomorrow at eight o'clock. If you don't show, I will get a warrant and have Bass here come and fetch the both of you."

Howard shook his head that he understood, and his wife, who was now starting to lose color in her face again, said, "I'll make sure he's there."

It was more than evident that she had no desire to see Bass return to her home, especially with a warrant that gave him the right to enter.

Bennet and Bass mounted and headed back toward the office. They visited as they rode about what each had accomplished.

Bennet said, "What the hell was you shootin' at? When that gun went off, I thought Howard and his wife both were gonna piss themselves."

"I kinda thought it might make an impression on 'em, as well as help me in doin' what I think we need to do tomorrow. "Let me tell you what we should do tomorrow."

Chapter 21

The Inquisition

Howard and Ed Burns arrived at nearly exactly eight o'clock and entered the office.

Bennet and the clerk met them at the door. Bass was sitting directly in their line of sight, glaring at them as if he had the power in his eyes to look directly into their soul. He made sure that each time they tried to take their eyes off of him, that he moved into a position that made it impossible.

Bennet stuck out his hand and greeted both men in a very friendly manner. "I hate that I had to bring you gentleman in, but there are some things that I've got to get confirmed about the death of Mathews and the others.

"Now here is what we are goin' to do. Howard, you'll come with me, and Bass will take Ed in the other office. Then we're gonna compare notes on your stories."

As the instructions were being given, Bass rose to his full height and a broad grin covered his face. He folded his arms across his chest, making him look as menacing as possible.

Ed's eyes widened, and he looked back at Marshal Bennet. He nervously said, "Marshal, ain't there some other way we can do this? That man looks pissed off, and all I'm here for is to back up Howard's story."

"Don't worry. He has calmed down quite a bit since yesterday. He seems to be gettin' over the murder and castration of his uncle, as best a man could. Besides, I'll have the clerk go back with you and take notes. You know Bass can't write."

Bennet turned toward his office door and said, "Now come on Howard, let's get this thing over with. I ain't had my breakfast yet."

Bass stepped directly behind Howard, making him look even smaller than he was, and reached for Ed's arm, wrapping his powerful hands around his bicep and applied as much pressure as he could.

Ed's face grimaced as he let out a cry. "Easy, easy, I'm a goin'."

Howard's head whipped around as he saw Bass push Ed toward the back office.

Bennet said, "Come on, Howard. Let's get this over with."

Once in his office, Bennet said, "Now, Howard, I want to ask you a few more questions. Have a seat." Bennet pulled out a paper and pen, while nodding toward the chair that was across the desk from him.

"You say you and Ed were havin' a drink together last night. What I'd like to know is, how many did you have?"

"Marshal. I don't rightly know, but it was several."

"What was you drinkin?"

"Whiskey."

"What kind of whiskey, and was it in a bottle?"

"Hell, I don't know what kind it was — just drinkin' whiskey, and it was in a bottle."

"Was there a name on the bottle, and how big was it?"

Now Howard started to squirm in his seat. "I don't recall, and it was a big bottle."

"Was you in Ed's house or on his porch?"

"We was in his house."

"Were you at a table or jest settin' in a chair?"

"I think we was at a table."

"You mean you can't remember if you were at a table or not?"

Suddenly the building was filled with three rapid, but distinct sounds of something striking a solid object. This was immediately followed by a cry from the clerk, "Hell, Bass! Why did you do that?"

This was simultaneously followed by, "Damn, marshal! Get down here quick. I think Bass has killed Ed!"

These words were flowing out of the clerk's mouth as he pushed his head through the door of Bennet's office.

Bennet sprang to his feet and rushed toward the door, where he and the clerk disappeared from sight. They had barely cleared the door when Bass entered the room, carrying the club he had fashioned the day before at Howard's home.

He walked to the desk next to where Howard was sitting and placed the end of the club, blunt end down, where the blood stains directly faced Howard.

Howard shouted, "God damn, help! Get this crazy nigger away from me! Help marshal! Help me, please!" He was fidgeting in his chair, looking at the door and realizing there was no way he was going to get past Bass and to safety.

He shouted, "God damn don't hit me! I'll tell you everything I know. I didn't do nothin'. I promise." He had thrown his arms in front of his face and was trembling. "It was Ed that killed your uncle and that white bitch. It was Ed and some others. I was there for a while, but I left before it happened. Mathews got scared and started runnin' away, and Ed shot him. Why, I don't know, but they sent me after him to make sure he was dead. I had a hell of a time findin' him in the dark and finally traced him to the yards. He had run a hell of a distance for a man shot, and I finally got him close to the yards. I grabbed him and helped him walk a while. I didn't want him to die. He was a friend of mine, but he finally gave it up, and I just let him fall to the ground and went back to my horse and went home. That's the truth."

Bass slapped the club in the palm of his hand and stared down at the little man, who was now sobbing.

"Who else was there?"

Howard shook his head. Then, through his sobs, he said, "It was Ed and R.T. and, and, and Robert Blalock and some others."

"What others?"

"C.W. Gaines and W.A. Lamon. There was others, but I don't know who they was 'cause they had on their hoods when they got there. I swear to you, I didn't kill nobody!"

Marshal Bennet stuck his head around the corner of the door and said, "Will you sign a paper stating what the clerk and I just heard you say?"

"If you get this nigger out of the room, I'll sign anything you want."

"Good. Now, Bass, go back and take Ed to one of the cells while I finish up here."

Chapter 23

The Big Catch

Bass had received a warrant for four of the toughest and most troublesome mavericks in the area. They were wanted for everything from murder to horse thieving. He had made up his mind that his concentration on these no-goods would be time well spent.

Bass rode east, and as he traveled, he would stop and visit his many Indian friends. He'd ask them about his targets, but continually got no positive leads. He had become very concerned that this was going to be a dry run, something that totally frustrated him. Dry run was not in his vocabulary.

He therefore decided to simply find another target. There was an abundance of lawbreakers in the area and no need to get upset over not being able to find his quarry.

Bass pulled up to his friend Alben Leadingfox's house and dismounted. He knew that if anyone knew of skullduggery, Alben would be a source.

Alben came out on his porch and stepped down the stairs, as Bass dismounted.

"I've been hopin' you'd come by," Alben said. "Things ain't right here 'bouts, had too much traffic and too many things a missin' from here and my neighbors."

"What kind of things?"

"Mostly small things, like chickens and food. Seems that a feller can't keep his family fed 'cause others is a wantin' to live the easy life."

"Well, chicken thieves is a little low on my list, but Alben, if it'll make you happy, I'll keep an eye out for the feathers."

They both laughed and exchanged handshakes.

"No, Bass, there has been a lot of food stuff taken, and I jest think that some bunch is holed up, bidin' their time and needin' some vittles until they strike somethin' big."

"You got any place in mind as to where they might be holed up?"

"You know the Jefferson place down the road and close to the creek? The Jeffersons left a while back. Said it was jest too rough here 'bouts. I'd

Judge Parker & Bass Reeves

think it'd be a good place to holed up. Got plenty of water and a roof. Ain't none of us want to venture over and take a look, but you might find it interestin' stoppin' by."

"Alben, I think I'll do jest that. Might find a real passel of chicken thieves there."

They both smiled and shook hands.

"I'll let you know if I recover your chickens."

Bass turned and started down the road toward the creek. He let Lightnin' choose the pace. He was studying the beauty of the trees and wild flowers that seemed to grow no matter how violent the Territory was. He thought how differently nature survived compared to the struggles of the land's inhabitants.

As he neared the creek, he pulled Lightnin' into a thicket of trees and dismounted. He pulled his Winchester from the boot and worked his way through the cover toward the Jefferson place. He moved slowly and cautiously. They may be chicken thieves, but Alben's assessment of what the occupants may be up to was probably more accurate.

Bass selected a spot where he blended in with the leaves of the trees and settled down for observation. His position behind the house gave him a great view of what was taking place.

Just as Alben had assumed it was obvious that the house was occupied. It was small and in a state of disrepair, but there was smoke coming from the chimney and there were four horses in the corral behind the house.

After a few hours of observing, a man exited the back door and headed for the privy. He was packing his six-gun, and the way he moved indicated that he was leery of what might lay in wait for him.

Bass waited. Observation was part of his nature. Gleaning all the information he could had often been key for him to not only complete his task, but to survive.

The long wait was finally rewarded by the appearance of Jeff Wilson, a man he had arrested before and was one of the men who was on his warrant list. He knew this man well, but it had been years since their paths had crossed. He was a low-life who had progressed from simple, minor indiscretions to a full-scale killer.

Now was the time to strike, but he did not want to face four guns without some kind of edge. He had no posse man for back up, so he decided that diversion was the best way to accomplish his assignment.

Bass waited until it was nearly nightfall and slipped back to Lightnin'. He rode, this time with great haste, back to Alben's house. He got there just as the sun was setting.

Alben heard a horse approaching and was on his porch with shotgun in hand when he realized it was Bass..

"It's you. I thought it might be some more chicken thieves."

"No, Alben, I jest came back to see if I could get you to help me rid you folks of the problem."

"What can I do for you?"

"I'd like to borrow your team and wagon?"

"What you got? A load to carry?"

"If I'm lucky. Your idea was real productive. I got some fellers I has been lookin' for."

"If it will help get some scandals out of here, I sure don't mind doin' my part."

Bass and Alben hitched the team to the wagon, and Bass went to his bedroll. He pulled out an old pair of overalls and a tattered hat, and he quickly changed. He removed his polished boots and replaced them with a rundown, nearly soleless pair.

Bass then tipped his old hat and said, "Wish me luck."

Bass had studied the lay of the land while observing the house and its occupants. He knew what he was going to do and rehearsed it as he progressed toward the house.

Bass pulled the team and wagon slowly up to a fallen log. He carefully worked until he got the log under the wagon, next to a wheel. Then he got the wagon lifted from the ground.

Bass began to cuss and holler and slap the reins as if he were doing his best to get the team to pull the wagon from its immobilizing suspension. He made sure the occupants of the house were fully aware of his presence and had no doubt that he was forcibly trying to accomplish some unbeknownst task.

After some time, he pulled a bottle of whiskey from the back of the wagon and started toward the house. As he approached, he was greeted, quite unceremoniously, by one of the men.

"What the hell is all the ruckus?"

Bass kept his hat pulled down over his face, just in case the lack of light might not keep someone from recognizing him.

"Well, sir, I's got my wagon stuck, and I sure could use a hand with unstuckin' it. I's got a bottle of whiskey that I'd be willin' to give to peoples that might help me."

The man looked at the bottle, that Bass held high, and rubbed his chin. He then glanced back at Bass as he stood in the shadows.

"What do you need?"

"I needs some fellers to lift my wagon — it ain't got nothin' in it — while I whip my critters to get it off'n a log. It's stuck between the wheel and the bottom."

"Well, this might be your lucky night. We was jesta talkin' bout how a little whiskey would make our stay more comfortin'. Boys, I got us some whiskey if you'll give this nigger a hand."

The others walked to the door and peered out into the darkness. Bass kept his head down and used the cover of the darkness to prevent those that knew him from identifying their enemy. One said, "He sure looks harmless, and I could sure use a slug of juice right now."

They all agreed and walked out of the house. They followed Bass to the scene and looked at the position of the wagon.

"Bass said, "If'n you all'll get to the back and lift, I'll whip these lazy critters and get this done. Then you can go to the house and enjoy some fine drinkin'."

The group mumbled, but went to their appointed positions.

Bass was standing at their side with the reins in his hands. When they all had placed their hands under the back of the wagon, he reached into his overalls and produced his Colt.

"Fellers, I'm Bass Reeves, and you're under arrest. Now if you will jest keep that position, I will be relievin' you of your sidearms and askin' one of you to help me put these here cuffs on the others."

The silence of the night air was broken by every kind of cuss word that had ever been known to man, but they knew it was far too late to do anything but comply.

Bass retrieved all of the items from the house that might have been stolen and put them in the back of the wagon.

Bass headed to Alben's house and pulled the wagon to a stop.

Alben was already standing on the porch with his shotgun in his hand. He asked, "What you got there, Bass?"

"Got a load of chicken thieves, but they is really more than that. These fellers is wanted for more crimes than I can count, and I need to hold 'em here tonight and transport 'em to Paris in the mornin'. Would you help me? I got some stuff here that you can return to the people you know, but I couldn't save the chickens."

They both laughed as they escorted the four to the barn and secured them for the night.

Chapter 24

Father

The train pulled to a stop amongst the clatter and clanging of its bell. The rush of steam belched from its side as the final motion of the great beast came to rest.

Bass slowly walked to the passenger car and entered the train. He turned to enter the compartment and noticed a large man sitting in the second row. He had seen men dressed in this manner before and had wondered what they were doing in the country. His activities had prevented him from ever having a conversation with one, and he felt that this was his chance.

Bass tipped his large black hat and said, "Sir, would you mind if I took this seat?"

The man looked up at him and motioned for him to take the accommodation.

Bass took the seat facing the man. It was where he felt he would have the best chance of viewing the stranger and his reactions, if he could get a conversation started with him. He had learned a long time ago that you could read a person like a book if you looked into his eyes. He had no intention of missing this opportunity to learn about this man and his kind.

Bass sat and now was staring directly into the man's face. He could not help but notice the clarity of the man's eyes — they seemed to sparkle. His hair was flowing and lustrous. He had the demeanor of a confident man with a mission to fulfill.

Bass had always fancied fine clothes, and this man's suit truly drew his attention. It was made of fine linen and fit him as if he had just left his home. The sure giveaway that he had been on the train for some spell was the fact that his shoulders were covered by the gray tent of ashes from the engine that had drifted in through the open windows.

Of course, the most outstanding things about this man's garb were his white collar and the large cross that hung from his neck. They looked so out of place and so uncommon that Bass could not help but stare at them.

While Bass was taking great care to study the man seated across from him, he was being similarly appraised. The man's eyes scanned Bass and seemed to stop for periods to take in the silver star on his coat and the butts of his pistols as they pushed their way past Bass' jacket and into the daylight.

They both sat and analyzed each other. After a few moments, the preliminary appraisal had passed. Each seemed to be waiting for the other to make ae first move.

Bass finally asked, "Stranger in these parts?"

"Yes, I'm Father Depreitre. I'm on my way to Atoka and the Catholic Church there. I've never been in this country, nor anywhere else in this land. My home is Belgium, and I've been sent here by the church to see if I can be of service. I'm fascinated by the land and the people that I've come in contact with to this point, and what do you do my son?"

Bass was taken aback by the question. No one except his mother had ever called him son, and it was a great shock to hear it from a total stranger. It took a moment for Bass to gain his composure. The sound kept echoing through his head. The word "son" coming from this man had such an unusual sound.

Bass finally gathered himself and said, "I am a U.S. deputy marshal, and I also am here to serve the people. My name is Bass Reeves, but most people just call me Bass."

"Well, Bass, it is a pleasure to meet you, and you may call me Father," he said, as he held out his hand that bore a huge and magnificent ring.

Bass grasped his hand, and they exchanged a warm handshake.

However, the invitation for him to call this man "Father" had once more confused him. It was taking Bass some time to assimilate. He had never called anyone father. He had longed to in his early days. He had longed to on many occasions when he was seeking advice on the ways of life. He now thought of the fact that his father had been taken from him long before he was born. His mother's story of how she had been separated brought back memories of the past, memories that he had not brought forward for years. In fact, this was one of the things that had made his choice of work so rewarding. He had no time to think of his past.

"I'm sorry, but what part of the country is Belgium?"

"My son, it is not part of this country. It's across the Atlantic Ocean."

"That must a been a right smart trip. I have met a lot of people here in the Territory that have come across the ocean, but I don't think I have ever met anyone from Belgium. You speak better than most of the others I have met."

"They school us well before we are sent to minister to the needs of our parish."

Bass thought for a while, then asked, "Father, if this is your first time in this country, have you been told of the dangers here?"

"Yes, I have been fully apprised of the situation, but that is why the church is here. We are here to help bring peace, love and harmony to the people of the area and serve them in whatever their needs may be. We do this in Christ's name and his mother, Mary."

"Well, those are great thoughts and ideas, but there is many a man here who has no need for what you do and would have no second thought of making your life miserable."

"I see you wear those pistols to carry out your duties, and I have my cross and the Holy Spirit."

"Father I know that there's been many a time when somethin' provided me protection, but the final difference seemed to be what I could do with these Colts and my Winchester. Maybe it was some spirit that was guidin' the shot or some spirit that was providin' the rock I was behind, and if so, I'm grateful. But I would hate to think what would've happened if all I had was a cross to do my job. However, I have a friend named Pistol Pete that had his life saved by wearing a cross, so I guess in that case, there's little doubt that the cross was his protection."

"Yes, the Lord works in mysterious ways. Tell me my son, have you lost many friends doing what you do?"

"The count is so great it'd be impossible for a man like you to believe. Most of my friends have lived short lives. Most of 'em have gone out rapidly and violently with little time to think of where they was a goin'. But my mama has always told me that if you do right and stay right, that the Lord will take care of you in the end."

"Sounds like you have a great mother. I don't know that I could tell you much more than she has."

"Last year, I lost probably the best friend I've ever had. He was the Judge in these here parts. You may have heard of him — his name was Isaac Parker. He was a great man and a true believer in law and order. He not only was my friend and a friend to my family, but he had done a great job in helpin' to clear this land of the bad and unjust. He had hung a great many men in his life, and I was a wonderin' if you thought that he had done right?"

"My son, it's not for me to say what is right and wrong. I know that in the history of my church there has been many a death brought about because of man's differences. I try to help the living see that peace and harmony are what man needs, and I hope that they will be of benefit to him and his family. I don't judge. There is but one judge."

As the train continued its journey, the two men continued to talk of the land and its people. They exchanged ideas of what was right with the country and what needed great change.

All of their conversations were continually interrupted by the clattering of the track and the screeching of the whistle as they would enter small towns, but the most disturbing part of the trip was the smoke that would from time to time completely fill the car and make it nearly impossible to breathe. Sometimes the smoke was accompanied by embers, belched from the steam engine and a threat to clothes and property. In spite of the discomfort, the stranger continually looked out the window and appeared fascinated by the landscape.

As they approached a steep hill, the train slowed, and even though they were four cars back, they could tell the train was having difficulty making the grade. In the midst of this climb, the train suddenly came to a screeching halt. Even though they were moving at a slow pace, the application of the brakes still pushed the priest back in his seat and caused Bass to lurch forward. The suddenness of the stop nearly placed Bass in the priest's lap.

Father Depreitre had a look of wonder on his face, but Bass suddenly jumped to his feet and reached for his pistols. He walked with a sense of purpose toward the car door, pulling it open with one swift motion.

Just as he opened the door, he was face-to-face with a man with a pistol in his hand, pushing it directly toward Bass' stomach.

Bass never slowed his movements. His left hand brushed the pistol aside, and his right hand cleared his holster. In one smooth move, he brought the gun down on the bandit's head before the man could even speak. The invader hit the floor with a thud, and Bass retrieved his pistol.

Bass then stepped down the stairs and swung to the ground with the use of the handrail. When he hit the ground, he hesitated for a moment as he scanned the tracks from engine to caboose. There was no one on the outside of the cars, but he saw six horses tied to a tree near the tracks.

Bass turned and rushed back up the stairs. He now knew that there were five more men that he must confront. He turned to the right and pulled the door open to the next passenger car.

There in the aisle were two men going from passenger to passenger, roughly and forcefully relieving the startled, and sometime protesting, occupants of their belongings, forcing them to put their booty in a bag.

Bass stepped back and closed the door. This was no place for gun play. There were far too many innocent bystanders who could be hit in this confined place.

Bass grabbed the man he had rendered unconscious and threw him out the door on the other side of the train. He then stepped to the side of the door and waited for what might appear.

His wait was short. The door came open, and the two masked men stepped through. They were approaching the next car door when they heard Bass say, "Gentleman, I will take the bag, and you drop your guns."

They turned to confront their antagonist, and found themselves looking down the barrels of two Colt .45's, now pointed and cocked directly in their faces.

"Before you do anythin' foolish, know that I hardly ever miss, and from this distance, it is impossible. Now drop 'em.

The men complied, and Bass pushed them back into the car he had previously occupied. He grabbed a passenger and asked, "Can you hold these two? I've got a few more to take care of."

The passenger said, "Sure."

Bass pushed both men facedown between the seats, one on top of the other. It was a tight fit, making it nearly impossible for them to move.

"Now, if they move a inch, pull the trigger. It'll go through both of 'em, so each is responsible for the other's life."

He turned and looked at the passenger. "You'll do that, won't you?"

With a wide grin on his face, the passenger said, "Sure, I'd more than be willin' to." .

Bass looked again, satisfied that he had chosen a man who would comply with his orders.

Bass knew there were no passenger cars behind them, so his prey had to be somewhere in the front. He decided to take the bandits on head first. He entered the next car and announced, "I'm a U.S. deputy marshal. All of you stay on the floor. Now which one of you men is the most pissed off about gettin' robbed?"

A tall cowboy stood up and said, "I'm pissed that I didn't have my shooter or this woulda never happened. They got my month's poke."

"Good, take this pistol and go back and help the man I left coverin' the two back there."

He pulled the unconscious man's pistol from his belt and handed it to the cowboy.

"Now, the rest of you get in the seats or on the floor between the seats. It may get pretty bad in here."

Bass then walked to the door of the adjoining car. He pulled the door open and entered with both pistols drawn, only to see three bandits leaving the car, but not before the last one turned to see Bass enter. He lifted his pistol and let a round go. The noise in the car was amplified, and the smoke and fire were startling to the passengers, but the shot missed.

Now Bass rushed forward. He got to the door just as the outlaws had cleared the train and were in the open. Bass stepped to the opening and shouted, "Drop 'em boys. This is your only warnin'!"

Two of the men turned and fired. One of the shots struck the car at about the same height as Bass' head.

Bass raised his pistol and picked out the man with the bag full of the passengers' valuables. He squeezed the trigger, and the man fell as he was in mid-step on his way to the horses. The next man reached for the bag and, at the same time, tried to get in the saddle of the now spooked horses.

Bass again shouted, "It's over! You can join your friend or drop 'em!"

The furthest man from the horses dropped his gun and threw up his hands, but the other kept fighting to get his foot in the stirrup.

Bass now took aim and shot him in the right leg, making it impossible for him to mount.

"Damn you bastard! I nearly made it."

"Friend, there is a lot of difference in nearly and making it, so put the pistol in the dirt and have a chance to live."

Bass then stepped out into the open and was walking toward the captives when he heard a shot that hummed as it passed his head. He immediately turned, ready to return the fire.

To his surprise, the sidewinder, who had fired the shot from the engine, came tumbling out and hit the ground with a violent thud.

Bass looked at the engine and saw the brakeman standing there with a large piece of fire wood slapping it into the palm of his hand. There was a huge smile on his face, and he slowly raised the firewood to the brim of his cap and then pointed it toward Bass.

Bass smiled and returned the salute.

Bass took a rope from the saddle of one of the horses and tied all of the prisoners. He then appointed the cowboy to look after them until they got to Atoka. His next step was to go to the dead bandit and see if he recognized him, before he slung him over the horse and took them all to Atoka.

As he was turning him over, he felt someone approaching from behind. He turned and to his surprise, it was Father Depreitre.

"What are you doin' here, Father? This is no place for a man of peace."

"This man must have the Last Rights said for him."

"The what?"

"It is something I have to do so he can enter heaven."

"Well, I'd figure he shoulda thought of that sooner."

"My son, would you help me turn him over? I must do this."

Bass reached down and turned the man over. When he did, Father

Depeitre let out a small moan.

"You never seen a dead man before?"

"Yes, but I know this boy. He and I talked the other night in Oklahoma City. He said he was a Catholic, and I blessed him."

"Well, it seems it didn't last long. Father, you're gonna learn that this is a rough and tough land, and you never can depend on anyone but yourself. I am sorry to have to tell you that, but it's just fact."

"My son, I hope we can change that, you in your way and me in mine. Now would you join me as I pray for this man?"

Chapter 25

Benjamin

Muskogee was a bustling, thriving town with much activity stemming from the great trade center it had become and the activities of the Dawes Commission, which had been set up supposedly to assist the Indians with their land, but Bass saw it as a making of a mess. It had come along with other measures of trying to civilize the Indians, meaning turning them into white men. Bass had always thought that this was a very stupid move on the part of the government. He knew the people and knew that deep within them were a love for nature and a continual longing for the freedom to move and live with dignity. The white man's idea of dignity sure did not correspond with the thinking of most of the tribal members he knew.

Bass relished the fact that a great number of the businesses in Muskogee were owned and operated by Negro men, and at times, he felt that his many years of service to the Territory had played some part in the success of these businesses and the acceptance of the service that they afforded the city.

On this hot June day in 1902, as Bass entered the city that was now his home, he had an uneasy feeling. The people on the streets seemed distant. No one said anything to him. It just seemed that their eyes did not make the contact that was usual, and that people did not walk in front of his full prison wagon or tip their hat to him as they usually did.

As he got closer to the marshal's station, he became even more aware of the strangeness of the day. The marshals who were in the area appeared to instantly have something else to do as he approached. They either turned their backs and walked toward some unknown destination, or turned to each other and became in some kind of deep conversation that did not allow them to acknowledge his approach.

Bass immediately transferred the reactions to his present trip. He was wondering if the citizens of the town and his fellow lawmen had already received the news that he had once again been forced to kill a suspect in another bloody skirmish.

His mind instantly replayed the recent event to see if there was something in the past happenings that would be interpreted as unnecessary or more violent than the people wanted to accept.

He soon shrugged his shoulders, realizing that violence and its outcome were nothing new to the citizens, and they had nearly always given him great support. In fact, it seemed that the times he had to dispatch a violent perpetrator, the people seemed to be relieved that they would not have to go through some drawn out trial. They also knew that a trial might end up with the release of the felon. It had happened before, and many a citizen had commented, "Why didn't you just kill the bastard and let God do the judging?"

He assured himself that his fellow lawmen would not be judgmental on this issue because they all had faced men who would not come peacefully. The results were either the lawman died or he took out the resister.

Bass replayed the arrest attempt of the three members of the horse thief ring in his mind. He had caught them holed up in a dugout and had asked them to surrender. He had told them that he wanted to take them into face the judgment that they were afforded, and that he would not tolerate resistance.

The culprits had answered his demands with a volley of gunfire. He had again warned them that what they were doing was going to lead to something far worse than what the court may find, and again asked them to throw out their weapons and come out with their hands in the air.

From the darkness of the dugout had come a voice, "Yah bastard ain't takin' any of us in, and as a matter of fact, yah is gonna be the one that pays for yah messin' with us. There is only one of yous, and we is gonna kill yah ass. So why don't yah get on yah horse and get the hell outta here."

Bass had replied, "Boys, I don't run. I ain't never failed to bring people like you in, and I sure don't think this day will be any different. Now, come on out before it's too late."

Once again, they had fired at him, and he now knew that talk was useless. He cradled his Winchester between his forehand and the trunk of the tree, he had taken shelter behind, and sent two rounds into the door of the dugout. He immediately slipped two more rounds into the weapon and waited for the response.

In short order, the door came open, and one of the desperados bolted toward where they had their horses tied. Bass took careful aim and placed a projectile into the fleeing man's leg. He pitched forward, and the shotgun he was carrying flew about twenty feet from him as he went to the ground.

As the man headed toward the ground, he shouted, "Boys, the son-of-a-bitch has hit me. Give me a hand!"

Bass kept his eye on the front door, but rushed toward the man on the ground, all the while keeping his Winchester trained on the door. He had just about reached the man when the crack of a rifle came from the hideout.

From his hip, Bass rapidly fired and levered his rifle he continued until he was out of rounds, all the time getting closer to the fallen man.

The intensity of the fire had completely silenced the resistance from the dugout. He lowered his now empty rifle and stooped to retrieve the shotgun. When he looked up, he was taken aback by the fact that the fallen man was struggling to get to his feet, and while doing so, had reached for his sidearm.

Bass shouted, "Don't do it! Don't do it!"

The man's face was gnarled with pain, but he continued his move for his pistol.

Bass cocked the shotgun and pulled the trigger. To his surprise, both barrels exploded simultaneously. The blast hit the resister in the center of his body. From the distance of less than twenty feet, the double charge of buckshot did more damage than even Bass had expected.

Half of the man's right side completely disappeared, and his left side looked like his spinal column was all that was holding him up. He crumpled to the ground, and immediately, all that was left of his intestines flowed from his body.

Bass had seen many a dead man, but could not remember seeing a body so mutilated since his experience at the Battle of Pea Ridge when he had seen the workings of grapeshot from cannons.

Bass turned to the house and shouted, "Boys, I have killed your friend, and I sure don't want to do the same to you. But if you wanna continue this, I promise you that your gonna join 'im."

There was no reply from the house for several seconds. Then a voice cried, "Yah killet my brother. I'm a gonna kill yah."

Bass now had his right hand full of Colt, and he was standing at an angle where the men in the dugout could not see him.

He replied, "If you got a mother, you sure don't wanna have to face this world alone, cause that sure is what is gonna happen if you come out of that door armed. Thank about it."

A silence filled the air, and for several minutes nothing took place. Finally, two pistols and a rifle came sailing out of the dugout.

"We is comin' out. Don't kill us. We ain't got no guns."

"Well, come on out with your hands in the air, and don't make any fast moves or they will be your last ones."

The two slowly walked out of their hiding place and did exactly as Bass had instructed, except when the one brother saw the mangled pile of what had been his brother, he fell to his knees and started to wail, soon followed by vomit.

This had been an unsettling chain of events that happened two days before his entry into Muskogee, but Bass knew that word of what happened could not have reached the city before he entered.

After realizing this, he now was even more confused why he seemed to be shunned by the people he met.

Bass continued toward the marshal's headquarters and instructed his team to deliver their charges to the receiving desk. He entered Marshal Bennet's office and was even more surprised when he got the feeling that his boss was also having trouble looking him in the eye.

Bennet immediately started shuffling papers on his desk and barely glanced up for a moment before he quickly returned his eyes to the desk and continued his obvious search for nothing.

Bass stood and watched this strange exhibition unfold in front of him. He started to look around the room and even got the feeling he was going to be arrested or something of that nature. Now he was really starting to feel uneasy. What in the world was going on?

Bennet finally stopped his incessant shuffling of papers and looked up. He simply pointed to the chair in front of his desk, and Bass knew only that he wanted him to sit.

Bennet still was having trouble looking straight into his employee's eyes, but finally cleared his throat and placed both elbows on his desk. This seemed to calm the man, and he turned his eyes toward Bass.

"Bass, I have some bad news for you, and I just don't know how to tell you."

Bass sat for a moment, and then said, "Well, puttin' it off won't make it any better. Is it about my family?"

"Yes, but not what I would guess you would expect."

Bass said, "Well, what is it?"

Bennet again seemed uneasy, but pushed a piece of paper across the desk and said, "Bass, this is a warrant for Benjamin Reeves for the murder of his wife."

Bass sat in a hush. He started to replay what had taken place. He knew what he had heard, but was totally convinced that he had misunderstood.

Now Bass was the one at a loss for words. He at last asked, "This piece of paper is a warrant for my boy Benjamin for murder of his wife? Is that what you said?"

"Bass, that is what I said. I am sorry to tell you this, but he is wanted dead or alive. I have asked several of my deputies to go after him, and they have said, no. They all wanted to wait until you got back. I think none of them wanted to face you if they had to bring him in dead, and none wanted to offend you by acting too hastily.

"Bass, he has said he will not come in and that if anyone comes after him, he will fight to the finish. If he is good to his word, it will mean that he will be killed and probably kill some of my men. I know he knows how to shoot — you taught him. I am told he has a rifle and a pistol, so his words can't be taken lightly.

"Bass, we are in a great of trouble here. I suggest that you go home. You have been on the trail for over a month, and you might as well go and stay with Winnie while we figure this out and hopefully bring him in without any bloodshed on either side."

Bass sat silently, looking directly at the warrant in front of him. It was as if he wanted to believe that if he looked at it long enough, it might go away.

Bennet was caught in the moment. He sat silently, staring at the best deputy marshal he had wilting in front of his eyes.

Finally, Bass stood and walked across the room. He stared out of the window and reached for his mustache. He stroked his mustache and rubbed his chin, never taking his eyes off the brilliant sky that hung over the city.

Bass at last turned, walked to Bennet's desk, reached down and picked up the life changing piece of paper. He folded it carefully and put it in his shirt pocket.

"I'll take this and do with it exactly what it calls for. I will bring him in-- dead or alive. He broke the law, and it is my duty to see that the law is fulfilled. Tell the others not to worry, and that I deeply appreciate their respect for me in my time of trial. I have no desire to see any of them harmed in any way because of my short comin's. I have failed as a father. I have failed my own son, and I must make this right, no matter the outcome."

"Wait a minute, Bass. I don't expect you to go after your own son."

"You might not, but I expect it of me. It is my duty and responsibility, and I don't want anyone havin' to feel shame or discomfort for my failin's. I have shame enough."

"Bass stop for a minute. You have been on the road for a month, and you're tired. Go home and stay with Winnie. She needs you."

"My boy needs me more. He worshiped the ground that lady walked on, and I know he is a hurtin'. I don't know how this will end up, but I know that I owe him for the things I never did for him. I was on the road too much, and I guess I just failed him. It's a dark day, and I don't want to make it any darker.

"I'll be changin' horses and headin' out this evenin'. I thank I know where he is a headed, and it'll take me some time to get there. Please, have all the others set still on this. I promise you it will be handled."

Bass extended his hand and placed his other on Bennet's shoulder.

"I want to thank you and the others for the kindness."

Bass turned and, always faithful to his duty, went to the receiving station and made sure that all the reports were made and his charges were booked into the jail. When he finished, he went by his house and briefly visited with his wife, Winnie.

She knew the entire story, and she confirmed the events that had led to the warrant. She hated to see him leave, but knew that his attachment to Bennie was far greater than any argument she could make for him staying.

Bass got in the saddle later than he had hoped, but still knew that time was critical. Winnie had told him that one of the reports of the shooting had stated that Bennie had implied that he might take his own life. He was so crazy about his wife — it was hard to believe that he had shot her. However, Bass knew that Bennie and she had had many problems over the past few months. Bennie knew that she had been running around on him and had even asked Bass what to do. Bass's answer had been one of the reasons the father now felt like he had failed his son. He had told Bennie that he would kick the hell out of any man that messed with his wife and never give it a second thought.

The story that Winnie told had confirmed that that was exactly what had happened, except that the interloper had escaped after a good thrashing and, evidently, Bennie had turned his hostility toward his wife.

Bass knew the trail to the old cabin where he and the children had spent several different weekends together, while they still lived with their mother, and he was stationed at Calvin and working out of Paris, Texas.

He knew that all the children had expressed their love of the place, but that Bennie had been the most outspoken. As a matter of fact, he had made the statement that if he died and went to heaven, he was sure this was the place he would end up.

Bass had thought it funny at the time, but now saw it as an omen of things to come. That was why he felt sure that he knew where to find his son who surely was not only filled with pain, but must also be feeling as if the world had turned into some kind of nightmare.

Bass decided that he had gone far enough, and that if he was going to be as mentally alert as he needed to be, he should camp for the night and get some long overdue rest.

The next morning, he did not even fix breakfast, but saddled his horse and dedicated himself to the trail. As the sun got higher, he was approaching his friend's cabin in the Cookson Hills. He had not planned to stop, but the smell of coffee and the fact that he had not seen Wilber and his family for several months, made it a justifiable diversion.

Bass eased his horse into the front of the house and let out a holler before getting to close. The holler was greeted by Wilber stepping onto the porch with his shotgun at his side, but upon seeing Bass, his look of concern was quickly replaced by a broad smile.

Wilber stepped off the porch and greeted Bass with an outstretched hand before the deputy could dismount.

"My good friend, how have you been? It has been far too long since you have been to my humble home. Come on in. Carlie has some coffee still on the fire, and I thank she still has a biscuit or two left, you must say hello and share."

Bass dismounted and said, "It's good to see you, but I can't stay long. I'm lookin' for my son and thought that you might of seen 'im."

Wilber said, "So happens that a couple of days back I seen 'im ride by. I woulda thought he woulda stopped, but he jest kept on a goin'. Guess he was in a big hurry to get some fishin' done over at the cabin, huh?"

"Wilber, you havin' seen him gives me much relief. I was figurin' that would be where I'd find 'im. Now you've helped me settle my mind. I'll be glad to share some of Carlie's biscuits and coffee."

In the house, Bass tried to converse like a long lost friend, but his mind kept wondering to the task at hand. He did his best to share pleasantries and did get some information on crime in the area, which seemed to be about all he ever heard about from any of his friends.

Bass at last said, "Wilber, Carlie, I thank you for your hospitality, but I need to hit the trail. Carlie, the biscuits were great."

Carlie jumped to her feet and pulled a cloth from her apron. She placed several biscuits in the cloth and rolled them up, before handing it to Bass and saying, "Yah might need this for the road. I know yah always is a puttin' yah stomach last when yah is on the road. Jest take 'em with yah."

Bass placed his hat back on his head and said, "I'm goin' now, and thanks again."

As Bass proceeded he felt relieved, knowing that he had correctly chosen the hiding place where Bennie would be holed up. Even in his concerned state of mind, he still was taken aback by the beauty of the country he was traveling. This year had been perfect, with just the right amount of rainfall, and the earth was showing all of its appreciation for the blessings. But, he again wondered how such a terrible situation could have taken place in such a glorious time.

Bass slowly approached the cabin. He could see smoke coming from the chimney and observed Bennie's horse in the corral.

About fifty yards before he got to the house, he dismounted and led his mount towards the dwelling. When he got about half way there, he stopped and stood.

"Bennie, it's your papa!" Bass shouted. "Bennie, I need to talk to you!"

The cabin was silent.

Bass stood and again shouted, "Bennie, I am alone, and I need to talk with you!"

This time, he could hear what sounded like furniture moving, but no reply.

"Bennie, I know you got a problem, and I'm here to help you. So come on out."

Time passed. No reply was forthcoming.

At last, Bennie stepped to the door. His hand held a pistol, and the look on his face was a mix of fear, anguish and relief.

"Son, put the pistol down, and let's set on the porch. Remember all the great conversations we used to have on the porch? We need to have this visit more than any of the others."

Bennie seemed as if he was responding to the invitation, but he pulled the pistol up to his side as he motioned for his father to come forward.

"Now, Bennie, I'd feel a passel better if you laid that pistol on the porch and took a seat. I've got to tell you that I have a warrant for your arrest, and I aim to serve it."

Bennie kept the pistol at his side and even raised it to where it was pointed at Bass.

Bennie said, "Papa, I ain't goin' to jail. I did wrong, and I know it, but I ain't goin' to jail."

"Bennie, we need to talk. I know you're hurtin', and I know you had your reason for doin' what you did, but we need to talk about what we can do from this day on."

"I'm not sure I'm interested in what happens from this day on. I killed Mable, and she was the most important thing in my life. I loved her so much that I don't think I need or want to live past this day."

"Now, Bennie, what is done is done, and there ain't no relivin' that. The only thing you can do is go on with your life and make it as good as you can."

Bennie slowly lowered his gun and stepped to the edge of the porch. He stood for a moment and looked at the ground, he then stooped over and placed the pistol on the porch at his feet and squatted down, eventually sitting on the edge of the porch.

Bass closed the distance, finally reaching out and placing his hand on Bennie's shoulder. He reached with his other hand and lifted Bennie to his feet, wrapping his arms around him. He pulled his son to him and held him in his arms.

Bennie began to sob, allowing himself the comfort of his father's arms.

"Papa, I just feel like I have lost everythin'. Mable was my life, and I took it away. I killed her dead, and I know I shoulda jest walked away, but I didn't. I worked my ass off for her. I gave her everything I could. I worked every hour of the day and week just so she could have whatever I could buy for her, and all she did was mess around all the hours I was a doin' all those things for her."

"Son, I know you tried, and that is all you can do. I know you tried harder than anyone I know has tried. I just want you to know that I feel that I am at fault for all this. I never spent enough time with you boys when you was a growin' up. I never showed you how to love. I was a workin' all the time and know I failed you and the other kids and your mama. It has come back to haunt me. I was out tryin' to get other people to do right, and now I have three boys who has broke the law. I know it is my fault, and I just hate it. You know that I don't have much money since they tried to put me in prison, but I promise you that I will help you all I can to defend yourself in court. You know that you are guilty, but with a good lawyer, we maybe can come out of this OK."

"Papa, I don't know that I want to come out of this OK. I just want it to be over."

"I understand, but in time you will change your mind. The Lord will help carry you, and you will become better for it. Now, let's just set and talk and take our time. I'm the one that is takin' you back, and I can say when that will be. Let's enjoy the beauty that the Lord has given us, and when you are ready, we will go back, but not until you're ready."

Chapter 26

United Socialist Club

Bass had accepted his new assignment to the Muskogee district and had set about adjusting to his new location. He had bought a home, and he and his new wife had decided that this was going to be their final location. This was going to be their home for the rest of their lives. It had even been made better due to the fact that he was working with a great lawman, Uncle Bud Ledbetter. They had worked together in the past and had always had a great relationship.

Bass had been in the town many times in the early days and was pleased that it was such a progressive trade center with a large Negro business district. The church was a welcome place, and he and Winnie were more than pleased to be a part of the community.

Bass left the house with a new vigor, for the spring morning was bringing to life a new time of beauty and growth. The air was filled with warmth that announced the best part of any year. The winter had been harsh, and the feeling of the earth coming back into production was most appealing to Bass.

He headed to the barbershop. He had decided that a new haircut and a shave would be a great way to celebrate his feelings of a new start for himself, as well as a new beginning.

Bass entered the empty shop, and Sam looked up with a warm smile as he placed his broom against the wall.

"Bass, it's great to see you. I'd expected to see you in church tomorrow, but it's even better that you've come today. I've somethin' that is really botherin' me and had planned to discuss it with you."

Bass said, "Well, I've come for a shave and haircut, but we can talk while you're doin' that for me, right?"

"I'm glad that no one is here, because what I want to talk about what could be a problem for me if anyone knew I was objectin'."

Judge Parker & Bass Reeves

"Sam, what are you objectin' to?"

"There are a couple of guys that keep comin' in and talkin' to me and my customers about this United Socialist Club. They're wantin' me and the others to join up with 'em, and it's one scary notion."

Bass listened as he removed his coat with the attached star. He hung his coat and big black hat on a hook nearby, then seated himself in the barber chair.

"They say that they have the blessin' of Reverend William Wright, and that the Lord and the law is on their side. They say that if any of us Negro folk joins up, we've the right to one-hundred-and-sixty acres and can claim any piece of property we want and just take it."

"That's a damned fool statement, and you know it Sam. Isn't that Wright the feller that was here a few years back and had a group called the Tenth Calvary?"

"Sure was, and I know it's stupid, and I hope the others they is talkin' to know it, but I also know that they're lots of fools out there, and I'm fearful that if this notion gets in some of these people's heads, that some big troubles are a comin'.

"They say they have got about forty members now, and that they is all lawmen and can enforce what they is sayin'. They say they not only have the law and the Lord on their side, but Wright has gave them a conjure bag that they wear around their necks that makes them invincible."

"What kind of lawmen? Where did they get sworn in?"

Sam placed the white apron over Bass and started to work with his scissors as he continued.

"I have no idea, but they showed me their badges, and they sure seemed to thank they had some power to do what they wanted to do. They said that one of their members has already took over a house, and that they are goin' to use this as a example of how serious they are."

Bass shook his head and said, "If they are fool enough to believe all that rubbish and start somethin', they are gonna have to face the police, and I don't think Chief Kimsey is gonna take kindly to that, but if it happens, it's best that they put it down hard to take all the foolish notions out of people's heads."

Sam had finished trimming Bass' hair and had just laid him back in the barber chair. He had placed a hot towel over his face and was mixing the shaving cream when two of the men who claimed to be representatives of the United Socialist Club entered.

They both had smiles on their faces and proudly displayed their badges on the fronts of their shirts.

"Well, Sam, is you ready to join up?"

Sam continued to mix the shaving cream as he looked at the two men.

"Boys, I have no interest in what you're doing. I've heard what you got to say, and it just don't seem right to me. On top of that, this Reverend Wright of yours was here in town a few years ago and claimed he was representing the President of the United States. Theodore Roosevelt sent some of his people here to check out what was goin' on, and before you knew it, he had vanished.

"I just tell you that so you might think of what kind of man you is dealin' with."

Sam removed the hot towel from Bass' face and brushed the lather on him as he continued to talk.

"I don't want no trouble. I just don't think you can or should do what you are bein' told. I know you have told me that it is right and owed you and that you got magic powers protectin' you. But I fear that you've been bamboozled by a sharp-talkin' preacher."

"Sam, you're a very important man in this town, and if you'd join us, it would bring a lot of others in, and the more numbers we've got, the more power we've got. We wish you'd consider that. I think we could get Reverend Wright to make you a leader of the group if you did that."

Sam was running the sharp blade of the straight razor over Bass' face as they were talking.

He finally said, "Boys I have told you that I fear what you're doin' and sayin'. I don't want to be a part of it, and I hope none of my friends and customers want to be a part of it."

Sam placed his razor back on the counter and put a splash of lilac tonic on his hands. He then walked back to Bass and carefully massaged it onto Bass' face. He used his towel to fan his face and the sweet smell filled the room.

Bass stroked his face as Sam set him upright in his chair.

Bass looked at the two who had been talking and before he could speak, one of the men asked, "How 'bout you mister? Don't it sound good to you that you could become a member of our club and get land and property for free?"

Bass said, "What's gonna keep you from gettin' shot if you take someone's property?"

"We got the right, and besides, we got conjure bags that keep us safe, and you'd have one, too."

"Let me be the first to tell you that I know the power of the conjure bag. Let me also tell you that in all my years, I ain't seen anyone who will just give you his property just because you tell 'em that you got the right. Most people here 'bouts has worked hard for what they got, and I can't see 'em just givin' it to you without a fight."

"We got badges and guns and the Lord on our side, and we ain't afraid to claim what is rightfully ours and would like for you to talk to the Reverend 'bout it. Why don't you come this afternoon to Fond du Lac Street between Second and Third? We is gonna have a meetin', and you can see."

Sam, with one flowing motion, removed the apron from Bass. The deputy stood up from the chair and adjusted his pistols.

Both men's eyes grew bigger, and one said, "You look like a man we could really use. Don't you know it is against the law to carry a gun in town?"

Bass simply looked at them, then took his hat from the hook and adjusted it on his head.

While he was doing this, Sam took his coat and held it behind him so Bass could put his arms through the sleeves. Sam helped him pull it up on his shoulders, and the brightness of the attached star captured the attention of the two men.

Bass said, "I can wear these pistols anywhere I want. It is my job to see that nothin' happens to disturb the peace in this Territory, and from what I am hearin', you are 'bout to find out how seriously I take that.

"I'm tellin' you, you had better back off of your plans and go to work like everyone else to get what you want, 'cause what you are 'bout to do is gonna cause you nothin' but trouble."

Bass turned and flipped Sam a dollar, then walked out the door into the warmth of the spring day.

***

Bass had promised the kids of the area that he would come to their baseball game and was just stepping on to the porch when he heard a series of shots echo down the street.

He rushed back into the house and pulled his Winchester from the rack next to the door. He hurried into the street and toward where he had heard the shots. He was moving as quickly as he could when he heard an intense amount of firing. He could recognize both pistols and rifle fire.

Bass knew that this indicated a full-fledged engagement. He grabbed a horse that was tied to a hitch in front of a store. He mounted and whipped the animal into full speed toward the ever-increasing battle sounds.

He reached Second Street and dismounted. He was shocked at the size of the crowd that had gathered to witness this massive shootout.

Bass pushed his way through the crowd, and as he went he shouted, "Get the hell back! Get the hell back! You damned fools are gonna get killed! Get the hell back!"

He turned the corner and saw Uncle Bud Ledbetter and Paul Williams firing from behind a telephone pole.

Ledbetter fired, and one of the Negroes on the front porch pitched forward. Ledbetter raised his pistol to fire at the remaining man, who was now crouching and taking direct aim at him. However, when Ledbetter pulled the trigger, the gun misfired.

In the same instant Bass, pulled the trigger of his Winchester, and the man on the porch fell back with a hole in his head.

The upstairs window then came alive with both rifle and pistol fire. Two bystanders were hit, and Bass pulled one of them back behind the corner of the building. He comforted the man for a few moments as the upper part of the building continued to rain a hail of bullets at the officers on the ground.

Bass stepped next to a man who was peering around the corner of the building and said, "Which window is most of the firing comin' from?"

The man pointed to the middle window, and Bass took aim at that window. In a moment, a man stuck his rifle out, and Bass pulled the trigger. The man dropped the rifle and fell back inside the room. In a short time, the house became silent, and the occupants of the house threw their guns out and walked out with their hands in the air.

Bass cautiously turned the corner, keeping his eye on the house and the people standing in front as he worked his way down to where "Uncle Bud" and Paul Smith were now standing. They were both reloading their pistols while keeping an eye on the house. Other officers were cuffing the members of the United Socialist Club.

Bass said, "You fellers alright? You been hit?"

Paul turned and said, "No, we're fine."

Ledbetter stood for a moment and looked at the crowd that was now moving about and talking in groups. Then he said, "You know, I'm glad both of you are Negro. Can you imagine the uproar that we could get from the Negro community if all this killin' and shootin' had been at the hands of white men? We could be in for a race riot — and still may be."

Bass said, "Bud, your right. I think that Paul and I should start right now and walk through the community and see if we can keep the people calm."

Bud said, "That is a good idea. Why don't you get R.C. Cotton to go with you. Stay together and make sure you come by the jail this evenin'. I fear the trouble ain't over, and there may be an attempted lynchin' tonight. I hope I'm wrong, but I would rather have all of the Negro officers there that I can have."

R.C., Paul and Bass walked through the Negro area and visited with everyone they met. They were more than pleased that most people were happy that the United Socialist Club had been put out of business. They in general felt that the blatant and aggressive attitudes of the members had enraged the white citizens and made their lives more difficult.

That evening, all three of the officers reported to the jail. Just as Ledbetter had suspected, a large crowd gathered and lynching was being mentioned. Amazingly, the crowd was mixed with many Negro citizens just as set on mob law as white citizens.

Ledbetter made sure that the three Negro officers were visible to the crowd, and that white deputy marshal accompanied each. After a few hours of tension, the crowd dispersed.

Chapter 27

Muskogee

Bass always made his rounds keeping a keen eye out for problems. This practice had enabled him to bring as much peace and harmony to the most troubled area of town as the violent history for which it was known. He knew he had been put here just for that purpose, and, in spite of his advanced years, he felt it a plan that worked well.

One of the reasons for his success was because of his long reputation of dealing with offenders. When he was assigned to an area, word traveled fast that he was a man not to be trifled with. This was reinforced with the swift action that he took on his first few weeks of an assignment.

Tonight was no exception. Bass exited his buggy and stepped on the boardwalk. His cane made its usual tapping sound as he strolled toward Jake's Restaurant. The tapping sound had come along with his reputation. Those who cared to break the law had soon learned that the sound was fair warning that the man with the big, black hat was on his way, and if they had any sense, they would alter their ways.

He entered the establishment that was known as the breeding ground for much of the district's problems, but first he checked his shoulder holster, making sure that it was secure and ready in the event it might be needed. All of his preparation was now second nature — all of his years had equipped him for survival.

When he entered, he glanced at the owner who immediately nodded his head, then turned it and gave a warning glance in the direction of a tall and stoutly built young man who had placed himself in the middle of the room and was taking great delight in being the center of attention.

Bass stood silently and observed. There was no reason for quick action, and he knew that the more he could learn from watching the man, the easier it would be to deal with the situation.

After some moments, the young man was raising his voice louder and expressing his great prowess, when his eye finally turned in the direction of Bass and the others standing at the side of the room. He could tell by the look on Bass' face that here was a man who was not impressed with his antics — and possibly the man he was looking for.

Bass laid his cane on the table next to him and straightened his tie. He then tilted his hat back on his head and narrowed his eyes as he stared at the increasingly belligerent young man.

Their eyes made contact, and for a moment, all of the commotion stopped. The rest of the occupants displayed an uneasiness, but sat transfixed, knowing that they were about to witness something that could be a subject of conversation for several days.

The silence was broken when the loud-mouthed youth pushed his hat back on his head and said, "Well, I guess you're the old bastard I've been hearin' about. They tell me you're one bad ass, but from the looks of you, I'd guess that was some time back."

Bass responded, "Young man, I have a job to do, and may I remind you that I've done it for years. I have faced many a man, most of whom were a greater threat than you, and I'm still standin' and still goin' about my business. I don't know what you've got on your mind, but you need to rethink whatever it is."

As he said this, he brushed back his coat in a swift and smooth move with his left hand, and the tail seemed to automatically cradle behind his pistol on his left hip.

Bass paused. "I can see you are upset, and you act like you want to prove somethin', but there ain't nothin' for you to prove, except what a fool you are."

Bass lifted his right hand up to the left collar of his coat and grasped his lapel just inches from his shoulder holster.

"Now I see you're carin' iron, and that ain't allowed in town. So, the first thing you should do is lift it with your fingers and lay it gently on the table."

Now the mood of the patrons started to change. They had thought they were going to witness this whippersnapper get the hell knocked out of him, and now they realized that it could end up being a gunfight, and they wanted no part of it.

Some started to scoot their chairs as far away as possible. Several, that had path to an exit took it rapidly. In a moment of panic, several jumped to their feet and rushed to the wall opposite the door, fearing that if they tried for the door, they could be behind Bass and caught in an exchange between the two men.

The youngster appeared to be stimulated by the fear and commotion he had caused. A grin slowly came across his face, and he flexed his right hand several times.

Bass asked, "Young feller, you got a girl friend?"

"Yeah, what the hell has that got to do with it?"

"Well, I was just hopin' that you'd tell me her name so I can explain to her why I had to kill you."

"So, yah really think yah can take me?"

"Friend, I have no doubt, and at this moment, you should start gettin' some doubts in your own head, for your own good."

"The way I see it, yah is old and slow, and I could surely beat yah. It sure'd be a feather in my cap when I do."

"And a great loss to your Mama and your girlfriend if you don't," added Bass.

Those at the wall were now hugging it as if they wished they could press themselves through the barrier and into the back alley.

Bass said, "Friend, I have all the notches I want, but if you insist, there's always room for one more. Now, for the last time, lay the pistol on the table. You're only gonna spend a night in jail, and that sure beats lyin' in the cold ground from now to eternity."

The hellion was not convinced. He again flexed his right hand and broadened his stance.

Bass knew he had done all he could to avoid this unwanted encounter. He had faced too many men not to recognize the actions that were being displayed in front of him.

Bass briskly released his lapel and grasped the Browning 7.65 mm in his should holster. He drew it so rapidly and smoothly that the youngster barely had time to place his hand on the handle of his pistol. The semi-automatic was pointed squarely between the man's eyes.

The challenger's eyes suddenly went from their former squint to eyes as big as saucers. His mouth fell open. He let out a grunt and instantaneously threw both hands toward the ceiling.

"God damn it, don't shoot! Don't shoot."

The room seemed to breathe one giant sigh of relief. It was immediately followed by a cheer from the assemblage.

Several of the men rushed to Bass and patted him on the back, but made sure that they did not get between him and the fool.

Bass said, "If one of you gentlemen will remove this man's pistol and bring it to me, I think this adventure is about over."

While a patron was removing the sidearm, Bass said, "Young friend, never ever think that age is a bad thing, because with it comes experience. You and your foolish ways have taken you from a night in jail to a charge of resistin' arrest and attempted murder."

Bass escorted the now dejected and somewhat bewildered youngster to Bass' buggy, then to the booking room at the jail.

Chapter 28

The Visit

The evening was just beginning. The district usually did not come alive until the grueling sun went down. Bass knew this, and his duties didn't start until he felt that he was needed. The district had nearly been granted to him exclusively. He had proven his worth, and none seemed to want to challenge him and his authority to enforce the law. The chief of police was happy; the merchants were happy; and the law-abiding citizens were happy. The only people who appeared unhappy were those who chose to disobey the law. The remedy for this was that they not come into Bass' assigned area, or mind their manners while there.

Bass had worked this part of Muskogee long enough to know that if he made his presence known, the word traveled fast. His reputation as a no-nonsense enforcer of the law had served him well. It seemed that only strangers or young fools were brave enough to trifle with the man of so many years of experience.

It had been a hot and miserable day. The temperature was more than one thought they could bear, but the thing that made it so uncomfortable was the wind. With every gust came the feeling that your skin had been soaked with water that was near the boil.

The sun was slowly sinking, and every inch that it slipped below the horizon seemed to bring about a reduction in the sweltering heat that had plagued the day. The flies that were a constant pest during the day would soon be replaced by mosquitoes that tried to suck the blood from you.

Bass sat in his usual restaurant, preparing for his rounds. He had no set pattern for his trips. He never wanted the citizens to know where or when he would appear. Surprise had been part of his success for years, and he saw no reason to change that. In fact, at his age, he knew he needed to always have an edge.

His coat and tie were part of his trademark and had been since he had started doing law enforcement. He saw no need to change his mode of operation. He believed that a well-dressed man immediately demanded more respect, and except for the times he had worked in disguise, he had always adhered to this theory.

The only thing that had changed over the years in his appearance was his cane. He had started using it when his legs started bothering him. He found that not only was the cane of assistance and, at times, a useful tool to get someone's attention, but it also was stylish.

Bass was preparing to make his exit when Anthony Washington came running in. Anthony rushed directly to Bass, and while trying to catch his breath said, "Mr. Bass, there is a man lookin' for you. He's a toten, and he looks like he could mean business. I heard him ask for you and came a runnin'. I sure didn't want him to get a drop on you. So I got here just as fast as I could."

Bass smiled at Anthony and said, "Boy, you are sure out a breath. How far'd you run? I would a figured that you were in better shape than that. I watched you and the others playin' baseball last Sunday, and you sure can hit that ball."

"Mr. Bass, I ran quite a ways. I missed you at your house and then missed you at the station, and I knew that there wasn't but one other place you could be, so I headed here. Me and the other kids sure don't want anything to happen to you."

"Well, I appreciate you thinkin' of me, and if I can help you in the future, you kids all know that all you have to do is tell me what you need, and if I can do it, it'll be done."

"We know, and I want to thank you for the ice cream on Sunday. We all liked it, and it sure hit the spot after the game."

"Now, Anthony, tell me. Did you see this feller and was he walkin' or ridin'?"

"Yes sir, I saw 'im, and he was a ridin' a big gray horse, and he had on a big brown hat. I think he was a Indian."

Bass reached down and patted the boy on the head, then shook his hand. "It sounds like you are about ready to become a detective. You did a good job, and I've got Sunday off, so I'll be at your game and cheer you and the boys on. Now, run along. It's about time to get home. Your mama will be worried."

"Mr. Bass, you be careful, and if I don't see you in church Sunday, I'll sure see you at the game."

As Anthony left, Bass smiled. He had worked with all the kids in the area and had tried to support them in anything he knew about. It was just like the old days. He knew that friends were one of the main sources for making his work successful.

Bass knew his district like the back of his hand. He had worked it as a deputy marshal and now as a policeman. He figured if there was some fool looking for him, that he could get the drop on him long before the scoundrel had any idea he had been spotted.

Bass took his cane and slipped down the street. He blended into the store fronts that were now silent. He walked to a place where he knew he could slip into a small opening between stores and just wait to see what developed.

As he took his place of concealment, he wondered who this man could be. Could it be someone he had sent to prison in the past, and they had festered their hatred for years? Could it be someone whose kin he had killed, and they had now decided to take their revenge? It truly didn't matter. Whatever was coming his way would come, and his only job was to be ready.

Bass' big black hat blended in with the dark shadows as he stuck his head out to observe the area. He observed several people moving down the street. Most were people he knew by sight, and they were going home for the evening or going to one of the gaming rooms in the district. But none of them were the stranger that Anthony had described.

Bass decided to wait a few minutes more and then start making his rounds. This early in the evening, not much usually happened. The reason he made this first tour was just so people would know he was there. He knew that his presence often kept things from happening.

Just before he stepped into the open, he saw the approach of a man that fit Anthony's description. The shadows from his brown hat made it impossible to observe his features, but he was on a big gray, and even in the dim light, it was obvious that he was carrying a pistol on his side.

Bass stepped into the total obscurity of his narrow hiding place and waited. If he could let the man position himself, Bass would know when and where to strike.

The rider suddenly pulled his horse into a hitch and dismounted on the same side of the street where Bass had concealed himself. After dismounting, he turned toward where Bass had so well blended into the night.

The stranger walked slowly toward Bass' position. He was turning his head from side to side and taking in all that surrounded him. He had the look and actions of a hunter.

As the man passed, Bass took his cane and thrust it through the man's legs while he was in mid-stride.

The sudden entanglement sent the man sprawling onto the boardwalk head first. He was cussing as he plunged forward, catching himself with his outstretched arms.

Bass stepped out to watch the man struggle to break his fall, then hit the boardwalk with a resounding thud as his hat toppled from his head and down the street.

As the man continued to cuss, Bass said in a low voice, "You lookin' for me?"

The man stopped his cussing and immediately rolled onto his back and attempted to sit up."You have found me, and that should be a plenty."

The man's face now was visible and he shouted, "What a hell of a way to greet a friend!" and broke out into laughter, while he slapped his hands together and rubbed some of the grime from them.

Bass smiled, and then began to laugh as he recognized his old friend Ben Horsechief. "Well, you should a come at a time with more light and not go sneakin' around and actin' all mysterious, if you'd wanted cake and punch for a greetin'."

They now were both in heavy laughter as Bass reached out his hand and helped his old friend to his feet. As soon as Horsechief was on his feet, both men stopped their laughter. They put their arms around each other's necks and patted their old friend's backs.

Bass said, "I'm sorry about that, but I got a tip that some ugly man with a gun was looking for me, and with my past, I couldn't take any chances. Well, maybe he didn't say you were ugly. Course, he's just a boy and maybe hasn't fully developed his senses."

These comments brought back the laughter.

Ben said, "Damn, I am glad to see you, in spite of the welcome. It has been too long, and I had got word that you were workin' for Muskogee now, and I got a break and decided that I'd come on down and just pay my respects." As he was saying this he walked to his hat. He picked it up and slapped it against his leg, then replaced it on his head.

Bass said, "I'm so glad you did. Ben, we shared too much to not have seen each other more, but I still can't believe you're here."

"You don't know how many times I have thought of you or how many stories I have told about you. In fact, I have told so many that people think I make 'em up. Let's go some place and visit."

"Wish I could, but I'm workin' tonight, and I got rounds to make. Got a keep these guys in check. I'll tell you, I'd be right proud if you went with me, and we can talk while I work. I'll go get my buggy, and you can tie on behind, and we'll go in style."

"Buggy? I can't even picture that. As a matter of fact, I can visualize you in one of 'em new fangled motor car just as easy. I would a thought that till the day you died, a horse would be under you."

"Ben, truth is, I've rode so many miles that I am startin' to come apart, and the buggy is so much more comfortin' to my old bones."

"Let's go get the buggy. I got it up by the café. Bring your horse, and we'll start from there. By the way, you need to put your pistol in your saddlebag. I don't allow guns in my district."

Ben said, "I'm a deputy sheriff up in Payne County, and I have my badge."

"Well, put the badge on and keep the pistol where it is."

Ben led his horse, and they walked the few blocks to the café. As they covered the distance, Ben said, "That's sure a fancy cane, but knowin' you, if you got a have somethin', it's gonna be somethin' special."

Bass tapped the cane on the boardwalk and said, "It's kind a become my callin' card. The folks hear it tappin' and either are happy I'm on my way or start a scatterin'."

"Do you really need it, or is it just some fancy thing?"

"I kind a need it. It just helps sometimes, and when I first took this district, there were several of the tough guys that learned that it could leave a whelp on 'em if they got out a line. In fact, I broke the first two canes I had. Seems that some of these fellers are real hard-headed, but this one won't break. I had it drilled out, and a steel rod run from top to bottom. Now I got a be careful with it 'cause it could kill a feller if I put too much in it."

Ben chuckled, "From what I've seen of you, anything you touch is a weapon. Remember when that old boy hit you with the chair and broke it to pieces, and you picked the leg up off the floor and knocked him colder than a ice cycle? I'll bet his ears are still ringin'."

Ben tied his horse on the back of the buggy, and they started down the street.

Ben said, "This is really a different way to work. I never worked in a buggy, but I guess when I get old like you, I'll have somethin' to look forward to."

They both chuckled.

"Pretty nice horse, but I'd of expected some big old stud."

"Ben, I know you heard about my murder trial. That thing liked to killed me. It cost me my farm, my horses and probably had somethin' to do with losin' my wife. 'Cause from the start of those troubles, things just got worse at the house, and after the trial was over, I had hoped it would get better, but it didn't.

"You know, when they divided up the judicial districts, I was sent from one place to the other. I really hated leavin' Judge Parker, but I was havin' trouble with Marshall Crump, and the Judge said it would be best. He still requested me from time to time. Even had me come from Paris to pick up

Belle Starr, 'cause he knew that I had worked with her so close in the past. She came along peacefully, but she didn't beat the law that time. He sent her up for a year.

"You know, I worked with her son Eddie Reed, and later it seems that there was a lot of talk that he might have been the one that bushwhacked her. I have my doubts about that, but I know they had some conflicts.

"After I realized the situation, I didn't mind the transfers. I'd always find a new bunch that needed settin' on. You know I went to Paris and to other places — even spent time workin' out a here.

"Was kind a gettin' back on my feet when we became a state. You know, most of the people were really happy about that, but us Negro folk had a really bad time of it.

"That was the end of my gettin' back on my feet. You know they put in those Jim Crow laws, and all of a sudden I had no job and became a second-class citizen. I was fortunate that after a while the Muskogee people realized that if they wanted to keep the segregated district in order, they needed a man of color who had experience and knew the town and most of the people. So I guess that my life once gain was shaped by the Lord. I fit their bill, and they brought me in here to keep control of this district.

"While I was out of a job, I had a visit from a guy up your way, name of Gordon Lilly. He wanted to be called Pawnee Bill. He had this Wild West show, and he wanted me to be in it. He offered me some pretty good money, but the longer we talked, I figured that it was more about me being Negro than for what I had done. On top of that, there was a lot of travelin' to do, and at my age and just getting' hooked up with Winnie, I turned 'im down."

While they were talking, Bass had kept his eyes focused on the stores they passed. He was always on the alert for any signs of trouble. It seemed to be peaceful, just an ordinary patrol. In fact, most people they passed tipped their hats or made gestures indicating they were either glad he was there or at least trying to show that they were not planning on causing any trouble.

They turned the corner, and from a dark shadow, a voice called out, "Bass, Bass, come here. It's Joe." The source of the voice stayed deep in the shadow, evidently to keep others from seeing that he was trying to give Bass information.

Bass pulled the buggy to a halt and using his cane for balance stepped from the buggy and into the darkness. He was there for a few minutes. All Ben heard was, "Thanks, I'll see what I can do."

Bass reentered the buggy and said, "That was one of my best informants, and he just told me that there was a couple of guys on the edge of town sellin' bootleg whiskey. It looks like this is not goin' to be a slow night after all. I'm glad you're with me. It should be fun workin' together again."

Bass slapped the reins on the horse, and they started toward the edge of town.

"I am out of my district now, but the whiskey they is sellin' is goin' into my district, so I figure it's my place to put a stop to it."

As they headed to the outskirts of town the moon lit their way. They soon approached the railroad yard and started under the railroad bridge. They had barley passed the shadow of the bridge when a shot rang out.

Bass slapped the reins down hard, putting the horse into full gallop. The next shot tore a hole in the padded seat between Bass and Ben.

Bass said, "Hold on. If we get to the other side of those trees, we can pull up and see what we can flush out."

Ben said, "I located the flash, and I know where they are."

"Good! Let's hit the ground a runnin'."

Bass pulled the buggy to a stop, and they both departed.

Ben said, "I'll head up through those trees, and you try to draw their fire. I'll try to get behind 'em. They're over behind that water tank stand. Send a round or two and see if you can keep 'em busy while I work around 'em."

Bass pulled his automatic from his shoulder holster and rapidly fired three rounds at the water tower.

His action got exactly the response he wanted. The foot of the tower became alive with pistol fire, and the accuracy made Bass seek the cover of a large elm tree.

He carefully returned the fire, hoping to keep the shooter in place. The moon was shining enough light that Bass could tell the shooter had not left his cover. So, Bass continued to send rounds in that direction. He knew that if he could hold them, Ben would soon get the drop on them.

While the time was passing, Bass started to wonder why a whiskey runner would shoot at him. First off, if he hadnt' shot, Bass would have had difficulty locating him, and the bootlegger could have probably slipped away. Secondly, why would a person take the chance of killing a lawman over a crime which, if caught, didn't carry that great a penalty?

While he was pondering the questions, he heard Ben call, "Bass I got 'im. Bring the buggy and come on over."

Bass drove to Ben's site, and it all became clear. There, with his hands in the air, stood Officer O'Kelly, one of Muskogee's finest. He was accompanied by Josh Green, a local man from the district who was often in trouble and known to sell whiskey.

O'Kelly said, "Well, if I had known it was you, Bass, I wouldn't have shot at you."

"Mike, you really expect me to believe that? You know my buggy as well as anyone, and besides, you know that I am about the only one who would come after you. I think you really tried to kill me, because you know I am gonna take you in. There is a lot of your buddies that would've looked the other way, but you knew I wouldn't, so you had no choice. But your buddies don't have to deal with the results of what you and Josh was a sellin', and I do. Besides that, I really have a problem with those who choose to enforce the law and then use it to cover their dirty dealin'.

"Right now it makes no difference to me. All I'm going to do is take you two to the station and let 'em deal with you."

They loaded up Mike and Josh, in spite of Mike swearing he hadn't tried to kill Bass and his promises to never sell whiskey again if Bass would just let him go. Finally, Bass turned to him and said, "Do you think that a man who took his own son to prison for life would have any kind of feelin's for a man like you?"

He then slapped the reins and headed for the station.

On the way, Bass said, "Ben, I'm sure glad you were along. Not just 'cause it reminded me of the old days, which it did, but because I think I would've had a time runnin' that far. I hate to admit it, but these old bones are failin' me more and more ever day."

They both chuckled, and Bass said, "I know it sounds funny, me who thought that nothing could defeat him, now havin' to state that these old bones just ain't what they used to be. I have been havin' pains in places I didn't even know I had. They tell me I have a thing called Bright's disease, and it will slowly get me. You know that's what got Judge Parker, and it sure put him down, but I think that most of that was he was just tired, and when they took the court away from him, I just think he made up his mind that his time had come. He had done all the good he could and didn't see any reason to stay around. You know, he just lasted about six weeks after they closed the court.

"He was one hell of a man, and I owe him a lot. You know he had my boy Newland work for him, and we stayed close even thought I was transferred to the Paris office. This place would of had a hell of a time becomin' a state without his work.

"Ben, you know he really had no good feelin' about hangin' people, but he knew it was the law, and it had to be done to clean up this Territory."

"Bass, you can give him credit and all that, but you had a fair hand in bringin' this place under control."

"Me and a bunch of others. One of the things that's so little talked about is the number of my fellow lawmen that gave their lives for this state. In fact, there were over seventy marshals killed within twenty miles of this place. I knew a good many of them, and most of 'em were good men with families and were just trying to do their job."

"Bass, they say you killed fourteen men. Is that true?"

"No, I'm sure it was more. There was many a man that I know I hit, and they probably died later in some place. Then, the one that I hated the most was the man I hung in Fort Smith. That is the only man I ever killed, outside of Bill Leech, and that was a pure accident, that has haunted me."

"How'd that happen?"

"George Maledon, who was the official executioner at Fort Smith, was called away for some family business, I think, and I had just come in from the Territory. Judge Parker called me in and said that there was a hangin' scheduled in two days, and that he wanted me to do the hangin'. I told him I didn't want to do it. I had never killed a man who hadn't tried to kill me or one of my posse first, and it just didn't seem right.

"He said that the man had killed several people, and he had to be executed on that date, and I was the only one there to do it.

"The Judge said that Maledon had already stretched the rope and had made the noose, and that all I had to do was put it around the man's neck and place a hood on 'im.

"I said that it just didn't seem fittin', and on top of that, I was scared that if I did it wrong, that I could either choke the man to death or pull his head off, and I didn't want to be any part of that.

"I finally said that I'd do it, but only if George would walk me through it and make sure that all was goin' to go OK.

"I did it, but even to this day it bothers me. It just didn't fit the way I like things done. I know he was no deader than he would of been if he had drawn on me, but it just never seemed right."

Bass and Ben booked Mike and Josh into the station and continued the patrol. The rest of the evening was peaceful, and they ended the night with Ben going to Bass' house for the evening.

***

The next morning Bass said, "Today is my day off so we can visit and just relax. Winnie has made us some coffee, and we can just lay back.

"I'd like to hear about you, Ben, and what you have been up to."

Ben sat back and cleared his throat. "Well, I continued to work for the Light Horse for several years and had some close calls. You remember when you ran into me up by Vinita, and me and my guys was after them horse thieves. They had us penned down and was really givin' us fits. The next thing we knew, you came out with them in front of your ten-gauge. It was a real life saver."

"Well, I guess it was just a repayment for the time that I was in about the same fix with that bunch of whiskey runners, and they had run me into a bushwhackin' that had me in such a state that I couldn't even get a shot off. You and your boys sure got me out of that hole.

"It seems funny how many times we have been close enough to come and pull each other out of tough spots."

Ben said, "Like you've always said, things happen that are supposed to happen, and it seems that there ain't no explainin' how or why."

"You know, we could go on for hours talkin' about these things, but I want to know about you and what has happened to you," Bass said.

"Well, when they had the strip run, I went and thought I'd see if I could get me a little piece of land and change my life, but I didn't get a piece. So I just hung around and finally got a chance to buy a plot when folks found that it wasn't as easy as they had hoped.

"You know from time to time, I run into Pistol Pete. He is as cocky and active as he ever was. Never misses a chance to show his pistol skills, and he doesn't seem to be gettin' any slower or less able to wield that pistol."

"Well, that is good to know. Say, was he one of those scoundrel marshals who took advantage of their positions and staked claims before the run? I was never more ashamed of my fellow officers. They were given the job of makin' sure that others followed the law and used the position to line their own pockets."

"No. He bought his first claim near the town of Perkins, just across the river."

"Well, that is good to know. He played a big part in my early life as a marshal, and it is nice to know that I can still look on him in favor. Tell him hello for me the next time you see him."

"If I can catch him between wives or puttin' on a show, I'll sure do that."

"Any way, while I was a waitin', I got jobs with the sheriffs of several counties in the area, and they gave me the freedom to travel the area and find out who was havin' trouble gettin' on their feet. This paid off when I got a good piece with a creek bottom and some really good pasture.

"The real thing that did for me was I got to meet some real fine fellers, and we became friends and neighbors.

"One of these guys is as tough as any man I've ever met. He was a survivor of Gettysburg and Andersonville, which is no small accomplishment, but the real test was his comin' out alive when the Santana sunk."

Bass held up his hand and said, "I know about Gettysburg and Andersonville, but I never heard of that other thing. What was it?"

"Not many have, 'cause it happened at the same time as Lincoln gettin' shot, and the papers was full of that story, and all the talk was about that and the search for Booth.

"But the Santana was a paddle wheeler that the government hired to take the survivin' souls back home from Andersonville. They had put over two thousand sick and feeble souls on the boat, and the boiler blew up. The boat was on fire and either burned all those in back of it to death or forced them sick and weak into the Mississippi. Then the boat hit a sandbank and spun around so that all of those who had survived the first blast were bein' burned to death or had to go into the water.

"Of the thousands on board, only a few hundred survived, and old Jim was one of 'em. He is a God fearin' man and figures that is why he only lost a leg, but he figures that the Lord took that as punishment for him bein' a sniper in the war and for all the men he killed.

"Jim may not have but one leg, but he can ride and work as good as any I've ever been with, and he is the one that will sure come back with a kill when we get low on meat."

"That is a amazin' story. It just goes to show you that no matter what problems you may've had, there is someone that has had it worse and has rose above it," said Bass as he stroked his mustache.

"There ain't no doubt that's true. I got another runnin' mate that is about as interestin' a man. His name is Tatum. He was like you — born a slave and rose above all kinds of challenges. But the thing that I am most beholdin' to him about is he saved my hide from a hangin'.

"As I told you, I have signed on with the law anytime I need a little poke, and I was between jobs when I came upon some hobbled horses. I knew they were stolen, 'cause I had seen a paper on 'em when I was workin' with the Pawnee sheriff. I staked out the area and hoped to catch the thieves when they came back for 'em. No one showed, and I figured the least I could do was take 'em to the sheriff and let him handle it.

"On the way back, two fellers jumped out from behind some brush and had the drop on me. I told 'em I was a taken 'em back to the Pawnee sheriff, and that I sometimes worked for him, but they didn't believe me.

"Before I knew it, they had my hands tied behind me and was throwin' a rope over a limb. I really started talkin', but it sure as hell wasn't workin'. They were just startin' to pick me up to put me in the saddle when Tatum rode up. He asked 'em what they thought they were doin', and they told him they were hangin' a horse thief.

"He said they were makin' a mistake, that he had seen me workin' for the sheriff, and then he advised 'em to let me go.

"They told him to get his nigger ass away if he didn't want to join me. He seemed to not take kindly to these words and hopped right down from his horse. Before they could even let go of me, he had his hand full of old Mr. Colt. And he took all of us and the horses to Pawnee.

"The fellers said they were sorry and asked for forgiveness when it was all cleared up. But Tatum made sure that they understood that if he had acted as stupid as they had, that they would be fertilizin' the ground under the tree where they were goin' to hang me."

Bass shook his head and said, "I can sure see how he became your friend."

"You bet your boots, and he and Jim have joined up with me and a couple of other old timers and are runnin' some beef together. We are hopin' to keep on growin' if we don't run out of time."

Chapter 29

Jim Webb

"Bass, I know you have had many a close one. Who, or what, was the closest?"

"Of course, Bob Dillard has to rate right up there. I chased that rascal 'till I thought my tongue would fall out, and when I thought I had 'im, he would just vanish like the wind.

"He was one slippery hombre, and of course, you know he nearly got me first. I gotta think the good Lord was on my side or my huntin' days would a been over the night I got 'im.

"There was a bunch of 'em that nearly got me, but probably the one that was as bad as there was and that got close enough that I can't forget 'im was Jim Webb. I think he was part Mexican. Any way, he was a short, dark guy, and he was mean to the core."

Bass reached for his cup of coffee and took a southing drink. He then placed the cup back in the saucer and set back in his chair.

"He ran the Washington-McLish cattle company, and all of his hands towed the line or he would put a beatin' on 'em, and if that didn't do it, he sure never hesitated to draw down on a body.

"His reputation as a bad character was around for years, but I never had no call to cross 'im, 'till he had a Negro neighbor, a preacher by the way, who had a small ranch, with his church right in the middle of it.

"One day the preacher Steward was burnin' off a spot, and the fire got out a hand and went on over to the Washington ranch. It burned a big hunk of their grass, and Webb was fit to be tied. They was gonna have to sell a bunch a cows that they had planned on keepin', 'cause they didn't have enough grass for the winter.

"I'm sure it was a accident, and I'm sure the old preacher was really sorry, but Webb took it personal.

"Anyway, Webb went over to the preacher's, and I guess they had one hell of a meetin'. I'm sure that on top of it all, Webb's language was insultin' to the preacher, and at some point, Webb just pulled out his gun and sent the preacher to the land he had been talkin' 'bout all those years."

Bass shook his head. You'll have to excuse me I got a go to the privy. It seems like that is about all I do anymore."

Bass returned and took his seat. He adjusted his chair and continued.

"I had a warrant for 'im, and me and my posse man Floyd Wilson went to get 'im. We knew it wasn't gonna be easy, so we both slipped into old beat-up cowpuncher clothes, and I changed horses. We rode casual into the headquarters, and there he stood. I know him from the description I had. He was with a guy named Frank Smith and the cook.

"When we got there, we told 'em we was comin' from Texas and was lookin' for work and was hungry. The look on their faces and the fact that they both took their pistols out and hung 'em by their side let us know that they weren't totally sure of our story, but they finally said for us to come in and the cook would fix us somethin'.

"I knew we were in a tight place, but we had to keep on if we were gonna have any chance of takin' this feller. Webb stayed close to us, way too close for comfort, and he kept eyein' us like he just was waitin' for us to make a move."

Bass tapped his cane on the floor and seemed to be concentrating on the spot where he was tapping. He then looked back up at Ben and said, "I don't mind tellin' you, I was startin' to get real concerned about the spot we were in. With Webb and Smith both still havin' their pistols out and stayin' so close to us that we were nearly havin' to take turns breathin', things were gettin' tense.

"I started talkin' a blue streak about cows, horses, ranches I'd supposedly worked on, and anything else I could think of. Floyd would chime in from time to time, and finally Webb seemed to relax a little. I hoped he would put his gun away, but that didn't happen. The only feelin' of security was that they hadn't demanded ours.

"Finally, I told him that I needed to tend to the horses, and he said that'd be fine, except he followed me to the barn. I fed the horses and went about my business and even pulled my Winchester out of the boot and leaned it against the barn wall.

"I was sure hopin' that would ease his mind, but it didn't work.

"We went back to the house. Ben, it was one of those that has a bunkhouse on one side and a eatin' room on the other, with a big old dog run between the two rooms, and a kitchen on the end. When we got back, I went in the eatin' room, and Floyd and Smith was still at the table. They were visitin', but Smith still had his gun out of his holster.

"Webb and Smith finally walked out in the dog run and started talkin' low and soft. At times, they looked in the room at us, and I knew in my bones that we were about to have a showdown. I told Floyd that it was about time to make a play or we might not get out of this place alive. I told him when I made my move, for him to take Smith, and I'd handle Webb.

"Webb motioned for use to come out into the dog run, and we went along. There was a long bench there, and we just casually walked out and took a seat.

"Webb was standin' about five feet in front of me, and I just knew time was up. I turned toward the kitchen and hollered, 'Cookey, that was about the most awful a meal as I has ever had, but I thank you for not poisonin' us.'

"You could hear pots and pans a clatterin', and he ran and stuck his head out the door, and said, 'You son-of-a-bitch! I hope they kill your stinkin' ass!'

"Both Webb and Smith turned toward the cook, and I knew that I had to make a move.

"I jumped and slammed my fist into Webb's pistol hand. I hit is as hard as I have ever hit anything, and the pistol went a flyin'. I grabbed his throat with my left hand and put all the strength I had in the squeeze. I had 'im against the wall and now off the floor. I pulled my pistol and nearly shoved it down his gaspin' throat. He had hold of my grip with both of his hands, and his eyes were a buggin' out, but he was able to gurgle out, 'No more!'

"The next thing I knew, Smith fired two rounds right at me. He wasn't fifteen feet away, and I couldn't believe that he'd missed.

"I pulled my pistol from Webb's face and wheeled and fired. Smith grabbed his stomach and dropped his pistol as he hit the floor.

"I don't know why Floyd hadn't taken care of him, but I know that the Lord must a known it was gonna happen and caused the shots to miss.

"We hooked up a team and loaded both in the back. Smith was hurt real bad, and he didn't last the trip.

"We put Webb in the jail. I'd done my job, and now the Judge would take it from there."

Ben said, "That sure was a close one, and I don't see how Smith missed you. I guess you're right — somethin' was just a lookin' out for you. But Bass, it seems that somethin' is always savin' you. I'll bet you were glad it was over."

"Well, by all rights, it should a been over, but Webb had some might powerful friends workin' for that big cattle company, and while he was in jail for a year, some of those friends got him out on a bond of seventeen thousand dollars. When his case came up, he never showed.

"I was fit to be tied. The murderin' bastard had killed a preacher and had tried to kill me. He had no rights to be runnin' free. I set my sights on gettin' 'im and makin' 'im pay. So I put the word out, and sure 'nough, he was finally spotted at the Bywater's general store over by the Arbuckles, on the whiskey trail. This seemed strange to me, 'cause Bywater is one of the fellers that put up the seventeen thousand, and he had lost it. I was havin' trouble thinkin' that with a loss like that, that he would have sure been pissed at Webb, but I guess they had some kind a plan where he was gonna pay it back."

Ben shook his head. "If I'd a lost that kind a money, I know I would a been pissed."

Bass looked at the ceiling, and then worked his cane back and forth on the floor, with both hands on top of the head and his chin resting on them. He was evidently replaying these events, and the memories were starting to come back clearer, or he was thinking of all the close calls he'd had and how it seemed that divine intervention had saved him.

"As soon as I got the word, I headed that way with Jim Cantrell as my posse man. We got there, and I sent Jim down to check it out. Didn't want to play my hand unless we were sure. Jim spotted him right off, settin' in a chair in the store, and signaled me to come on.

"When I got there, he must have been expectin' somethin' 'cause he jumped out the window with both his rifle and pistol. He rolled to his feet and hightailed it toward his horse. I laid down on my horse and cut him off. He turned and was hoofin' it at full speed toward a clump of trees, about six hundred yards away.

"I decided to let him run it out, and when he got winded, he would be a lot easier to handle. If his strugglin' for air bothered him, it sure wasn't shownin'. He fired on me, and the bullet creased my saddle horn. I was hopin' this was a lucky shot, but the next one I felt go across my chest. Later I found it took a button off a my shirt. He was gettin' too close, so I headed toward some cover.

"He let go with another round, and damned if he didn't cut both reins just below my hands. I rolled off my horse and hit the ground, and before I could get my footin', he fired again. This one took my hat off.

"I was a thinkin', he has hit all around me. Sure 'nough he's gonna find the center if I don't do somethin' about it.

"I took my aim and hoped that I could get my shot off before he got lucky. He was at least five hundred yards away, and I had to allow for the wind and distance. I sent him a round, and he stood for a second, so I sent him another. This time he hit the ground.

"Cantrell and Bywater were there by the time I walked down to where he was layin'. He had his pistol in his hand, so I guess he'd run out of bullets for his Winchester. I kept a bead on him as I approached, and when I got close, he said, 'Bass, you are one brave man. I want you to take my pistol and scabbard, as a present. You gotta take it. I've killed eleven men with it, four of 'em in Indian Territory, and I was plannin' on makin' you the twelfth.'

"I took it and still have it in the closet. I don't know if it made 'im happy or sad, but it was what he wanted. He passed on pretty quick after that, and I found I had hit him both times, just a few inches apart."

"Damn, Bass, there is no doubt that you is bein' looked after. Maybe, you got some of that Cherokee medicine when you were a livin' there. No matter what it is, it sure is workin'."

"Well, sometimes that medicine works both ways. As a matter of fact, it came as close to takin' me out as any scoundrel or bullet I have ever faced."

"What'd you mean?"

"A few years back I was havin' a real lucky streak and had filled two wagons with prisoners. I was up by North Fork and had a bunch of horsethieves in my sights. Two of 'em was Indians, and they had given a medicine man named Yah-kee a horse to get him to make medicine so that I couldn't see 'em. That invisible stuff didn't work. I got 'em, and while I was loadin' 'em, they went to complainin' that they were supposed to be invisible, and that Yah-kee had failed 'em.

"I had a warrant for 'im also and asked 'em where he was. They were so upset that the medicine hadn't worked that they flat out told me.

"I went and picked him up with no problem and brought him to the wagon, and we started toward Fort Smith. I had a big number, and it was goin' to be a very profitable trip.

"The trip should've been the least of my problems, but as we moved on, I started to feel real bad. It seemed that the farther we went, the worse I felt. I was hurtin' from the top of my head to the bottom of my feet. Stiff and sore and pains that felt like my whole insides were on fire. I could barely set in the saddle. In fact, I had pulled my horse up so short that I couldn't keep up with the wagons. By the time I caught up with 'em, they had already eaten, and the prisoners were all chained and takin' a nap under a shade tree.

"I was hurtin' so bad I could barely get off my horse. My eyes were swollen nearly shut, and my bones felt like they were gonna come out of my body. I stumbled and fell to the ground and crawled to the shade of the tree. It took me some time just to get my breath back from the crawl.

"I just couldn't believe how bad I felt and finally decided that it was my time to go.

Two fisted justice

"My cook brought me some food and water.

"The look on his face told me that I looked as bad as I felt. As a matter of fact, he only put what he brought on the ground next to me. Figure he didn't want to get too close.

"I couldn't eat, but I drank every drop of the water, and all I could think about was that I didn't think my thirst would be very satisfied.

"I'd seen the power of the medicine men when I lived in the Territory, but I'd never had it used on me. Now, I was sure that the damned medicine man had decided to put me away. I didn't know what I was gonna do, but knew that if I wanted to live, I'd better do somethin'.

"I finally pulled together my last bit of strength, and despite the pain, crawled to where Yah-kee was sleepin'. I don't know if I was goin' there to beg for help or what. I just felt that he was the cause of my problem, and I had to get close to 'im.

"As I was reachin' for 'im, I saw his jacket pocket was open, and I could see a string comin' out of his coat pocket. I pulled on it, and his conjure bag was attached to it. The buck-skin bag was filled with stones, herbs, a lot of hair, dried berries and roots. There were clumps of hair in different sizes and colors, and a string was tied around each bunch.

"I pulled the bag out, and with all the strength I had left, threw that bag in the creek that ran by the camp.

The bag had no sooner than hit the water when Yah-kee woke and nearly jumped to his feet all in one motion. He immediately said, 'You stole my conjure bag. Give it back!'

"I told him that it was gone and good riddance.

"He pleaded with me and promised all kind of rewards if I'd return it. He had the look of a child who had just lost his best puppy. He had tears in his eyes, and finally said that if I would return it, he would be my servant for the rest of his life, that without it, he had lost all of his power and could never take his place back with the tribe.

"I had no intention of returnin' it, and the fact that I'd started to feel better at nearly the same time as the bag hit the water made me know that his power was in the bag, and that no man could allow him to have that much control of his fate.

"In fact, my recovery was so rapid that within an hour I had a good meal and was back in the saddle.

"I will never doubt the medicine and its power. I just feel lucky to have survived it. It for sure was worse than any bullet I've ever faced.

"Yah-kee told me later that if he had had the bag for another half day, I'd a been gone."

Ben said, "You were truly lucky. I've seen the medicine work back home, and it is amazin' what these men can do with it. I know you were lucky. Luckier than you can imagine. I've seen several people die from the curses, and I'd never doubt their power."

Bass said, "I have always thought how strange it was that the only time I was sure I was goin' to die was not while facin' a gun."

"Bass, I keep hearin' a story about you walkin' twenty-eight miles to catch a couple of guys. Is that true?"

"Ha, I keep hearin' that story, and all I can think is that someone wants to paint me a fool. But you know, once a story starts, it is nearly impossible to stop.

"The real truth is these two brothers had a five thousand dollar bounty on 'em, and that would get anyone's attention. I had finally found where they lived and decided that I would do whatever it took to bring them in.

"I had my posse men set up several miles away and told them to wait for me. I took my old cloths out of the stash and shot two holes in my hat, put on some old run-over boots and rode my horse with two extras to about three miles of the house. I hid the horses and then walked to the house. I timed it so I would get there about dark and walked fast enough so that I had worked up a good sweat.

"When I got there, the boy's mother was there alone, and she came to the door. I told her that I needed some food and explained to her that my horse had been shot out from under me and that I had managed to escape the posse that was after me.

"She bought the story and gave me food. After we visited for a while, she said that her boys would be in that evenin', and I should wait and visit with 'em. They had a big job planned and would need some help.

"The brothers showed up about a hour later, and I told 'em about all the crimes I had been involved with, and they were pleased to have me with 'em.

"We went to bed on the floor, and when I heard 'em snorin', I put restraints on 'em and let 'em complete their night's sleep.

"When they woke, I marched 'em out of the house and toward the horses. Their mother followed us most of the way and called me everything she could think of. It got so bad, I was sure at some point she would stoop so low as to call me a white man, but she never did."

Ben and Bass both broke out in laughter, and Ben said, "Well, I felt for sure that no man would walk that far for any reason, and I am glad you cleared that up."

"Well, for five thousand dollars a man would do a lot of things, but a walk of twenty-eight miles was not called for. All I wanted to do was work up a good sweat, and the three miles did that for me."

"So, that ends that story. What about the story of you arresting your preacher? I guess that is a bunch of bull as well?"

"No, that really happened, much to my disappointment. Reverend Wilson Hobson was my Baptist preacher. Not only was he my preacher, he was the man who baptized me. He was breakin' the law, and I just can't deal with that. The laws are written to be enforced, and it is my job to see that that happens."

"I know you are a religious man, and that must of really put you in a uncomfortable spot."

"It did, and I really had troubles with it, 'cause he had been a great teacher for me, and I had great respect for him. But, it is my job to bring people in. It is not my job to judge them."

"Bass, what had he done?"

"That is the crazy part. He was selling whiskey to his members — now get this — in order to pay off the church debt. And the members had approved this manner of business.

"Ha, I guess I missed the deacon's meetin' the night they decided on that move."

Their recalling of the past went through the night and into the next morning.

As they drank coffee and ate eggs, the tone of the visit changed. Bass suddenly became a man who was very upset with Statehood and what it had done to him and his people. He finally turned and called Winnie.

"Baby, come on in here and bring me those newspapers that I had you save. I want Ben here to read 'em to me."

Winnie walked into the kitchen, wiping her hands on the apron that hung in front of her dress.

"Bass, you know all that does is get you upset, and it is too fine a mornin' for that. You two have been havin' a great time relivin' your past, and there is no reason for you to get all worked up over somethin' that has long past and will never change."

Bass said, "I don't care. I want Ben to see in print what has took place and why it ain't gonna change 'til some leader with some Christian backbone takes a stand. Now baby, please get me those papers."

"OK, but you know how you get, and it just ain't good for you to get all riled up the way you been feelin'."

In a few minutes she returned with some papers in her hand and handed them to Ben.

"Now, Ben, I want you to read that word for word, just like it is, and remember that it was written right here in Muskogee just before the Territory became a state."

Ben picked up the paper and unfolded it.

"Jim Crow law will be one of the first in the state of Oklahoma. Sept. 16, Muskogee, I.T.

When Indian Territory gets statehood, doubtless at the time the legislative convention will pass a Jim Crow Law, and that is going to cause a big howl from the minority population of the Territory. The negroes here, especially the freedmen, by virtue of being land holders, have brought themselves to believe that they are entitled to all the privileges of a white man. This will continue until some form of local self-government comes, and the feeling at that time is likely to be so intense that very stringent law of this character will be enacted. In railway coaches, streetcars and elevators, the negroes take equality with whites. Since the new railroads have been built into Texas and Arkansas where Jim Crow laws are in force, the negroes of the Territory have been given a taste of what they may expect in the future in the Territory, and they resent it bitterly, but the white population recognizes that there must be some such law to protect the public, and it is likely that both political parties will agree to such a bill."

Bass said, "They need some such law to protect the public? Who in the hell do they think has been protecting the public for the last thirty years? It was this Negro man that's who. Now, Ben, this was just the start. I got more for you to read. Go on now and do it. You know I can't read, but that cartoon should give you the idea of how this state and the people are making their feelings known about their stand on this Jim Crow thing."

Ben picked up the next paper. When he attempted to press the wrinkles out, it made a crackling sound as if the duo were sitting around a campfire. The cartoon showed three poorly dressed and exaggerated Negro children standing next to a well-dressed little white girl, in a waiting room of what appeared to be a train station. The headline read, "The Negro must be taught his proper place," and was followed by a statement that the races must be kept totally separate.

"Now, Ben, I know these are old examples of what has taken place over the years, but it has raised my hackles to see how all of my people fled here after the war, and most of them set up good farms and businesses, especially around Muskogee. They thought this was the promise land, and here they could live the life promised all Americans.

"But when statehood came, the constitution convention was controlled by damned Confederates. I'm told that over eighty percent of the delegates had pledged to put Jim Crow laws in the constitution.

"When it was found that President Roosevelt wouldn't sign the constitution making it a state with that in it, they submitted a constitution just so he would sign it. As soon as that was done, the low life rascals enacted law after law that took human rights away from my people and me.

"I just have a really hard time of that. There are over a dozen black cities in this state, and I have worked in all of 'em. The people there are no different than in any other town. It just goes to show you that the Civil War has not ended, and I see little hope that it will any time in the future."

Winnie said, "Ben, I am sorry that you have to listen to this man rant about all of this, but he just feels betrayed by the people that he served so well."

"Don't worry. I know how hard he has worked to make this a livable place for all of the people, and to see it taken away has to hurt," said Ben, as he looked at his old friend tapping his cane on the floor.

"Well, I spent over thirty years of my life and saw so many of my fellow marshals of all colors give their lives for this place, and it just don't set well with me," Bass said as he adjusted his position in the chair to help relieve his pain. It wasn't only me, there were many Negro marshals that helped clean up this land and one of the reasons, outside of it not bein' right, was the President Teddy knew and recognized that the Negro 11th Calvary actually played a big part in his bein' successful at the Battle of San Juan Hill.

Ben turned to him and asked, "Is that pain getting worse?"

"It seems to get worse every day. I know it is goin' to take me down, and sometimes I wish that one of those hundreds of bullets that were sent my way had hit their mark. I just hate it that I am havin' to go out this way. As a matter of fact, I think I have served my last days as a lawman and will hand in my resignation tomorrow. I just don't feel that I am able to do the job that I should, and I just plan to set here and let Winnie take care of me."

Ben looked at Bass for several minutes, and then said, "My friend, you were the best I ever rode with, and I have heard the same from so many others. You have the right to do as you want, and I wish you the best. This state wouldn't have been the same without you and the others you trained and served with. I want you to know that I hold you in the same light that I held Sam Sixkiller, and I want to thank you for all you have done."

"Well, it was a hell of a ride, and I thank you for your thoughts. It has been a pleasure to have you come and visit me, and I hope you will return soon."

Ben walked across the room and extended his hand.

"I hate to go, but it is a long trip back. If I can, I will return."

Bass struggled to his feet and threw his left arm around Ben's neck, then escorted him to the door. "If you see any of the old bunch, tell 'em I will miss 'em and wish 'em all the luck in the world."

Chapter 30

The End of the Trail

Ben made the trip to the Mankillers' homestead with a heavy heart. When he saw the Muskogee Phoenix that morning, he figured the Mankillers probably had not seen it. If they had, they would be in need of company.

He rode down the trail to the Mankiller home and gave the appropriate shout to announce his arrival, but the sound that came from his voice was not with the usual strength. The fact that he could get the cry out seemed daunting.

As he approached, he saw Sam and Lydia come out of their house and onto the porch. They were much older and moved slower than in the years past, but they held onto each other for support, and began to smile as they recognized their old friend riding up to the house.

Ben waved before stopping his horse at the water trough. He dismounted and slowly removed the newspaper from his saddlebag, avoiding for a few moments looking directly at the Mankillers. Then he hesitantly turned to the house.

As he neared the porch, Sam stepped forward and held out his hand.

"Ben, you old dog, what brings you to our humble home? It has been too long since you have been here. I hope you are well." As he spoke, Sam realized that his friend carried a sadness.

"Sam and Lydia, I come with a heavy heart, but you need to know what has happened."

"What's that, Ben?" Sam asked, a look of concern crossing his face.

"I have bad news for you folks. Bass has died."

There was a gasp from Lydia, then silence from the porch as Sam and Lydia clutched each other.

"My god, what terrible news," Lydia said.

Withdrawing from Sam's arms, she reached into her apron pocket

Two fisted justice

where she retrieved a handkerchief and carefully wiped the tears from her cheek. Then she grasped Sam's arm to steady herself.

Ben stepped to the porch and said, "I brought the Muskogee paper and want to read to you what they said about him. It is about the only way I know to deal with this news."

"Please," Sam said. "We would like to hear it. It would give us time to help collect ourselves."

> "*Muskogee Phoenix*
> *Thursday, January 13, 1910*
>
> BASS REEVES DEAD;
> UNIQUE CHARACTER
> Man of the 'Old Days' Gone
> Deputy Marshal Thirty-Two Years.
>
> *Bass Reeves is dead. He passed away yesterday afternoon about three o'clock, and, in a short time, news of his death had reached the federal court house where the announcement was received in the various offices with comments of regret and where it recalled to the officers and clerks many incidents in the early days of the United States court here in which the old negro deputy featured heroically.*
>
> *Bass Reeves had completed thirty-two years service as deputy marshal when, with the coming of statehood, at the age of sixty-nine, he gave up his position. For about two years then, he served on the Muskogee police force, which position he gave up about a year ago on account of sickness, from which he never fully recovered. Bright's disease and a complication of ailments, together with old age, were the cause of his death.*
>
> *The deceased is survived by his wife and several children, only one of whom, a daughter, Mrs. Alice Spahn, lives in Muskogee. His mother, who is eighty-seven years old, lives at Van Buren, Arkansas, where a sister of his also is living.*
>
> *The funeral will be held at noon Friday from the Reeves' home at 816 North Howard Street. Arrangements for the funeral had not been completed last evening."*

Ben, dropped his head and looked at the Mankillers.

"I know this is a hard time for you, but I knew that I had to share this with people who cared about and loved this man.

"I think it is strange that both Bass and Judge Parker died of the same disease, and that they both seemed to stay dedicated to their work until the end. Their respect for the law and each other is was remarkable. The fact that both put many a desperado in the ground will long be remembered, but the thing that most people want know is that they both were very much against killing.

"Parker told Bass that he only did it because of the law that he swore to uphold and Bass told Parker that it was his duty to bring the wanted in, anyway that was necessary.

"I just wonder if the people or the state of Oklahoma will ever realize what great men they were, and what an important part they played in making this place what it is today?"

Made in the USA
Monee, IL
11 December 2023